OECD Tax Policies Stud
No. 3

D0127443

Taxing Insurance
Companies

OECD

ORGANISATION FOR ECONOMIC CO-OPERATION AND DEVELOPMENT

ORGANISATION FOR ECONOMIC CO-OPERATION AND DEVELOPMENT

Pursuant to Article 1 of the Convention signed in Paris on 14th December 1960, and which came into force on 30th September 1961, the Organisation for Economic Co-operation and Development (OECD) shall promote policies designed:

- to achieve the highest sustainable economic growth and employment and a rising standard of living in Member countries, while maintaining financial stability, and thus to contribute to the development of the world economy;

- to contribute to sound economic expansion in Member as well as non-member countries in the process of economic development; and

- to contribute to the expansion of world trade on a multilateral, non-discriminatory basis in accordance with international obligations.

The original Member countries of the OECD are Austria, Belgium, Canada, Denmark, France, Germany, Greece, Iceland, Ireland, Italy, Luxembourg, the Netherlands, Norway, Portugal, Spain, Sweden, Switzerland, Turkey, the United Kingdom and the United States. The following countries became Members subsequently through accession at the dates indicated hereafter: Japan (28th April 1964), Finland (28th January 1969), Australia (7th June 1971), New Zealand (29th May 1973), Mexico (18th May 1994), the Czech Republic (21st December 1995), Hungary (7th May 1996), Poland (22nd November 1996), Korea (12th December 1996) and the Slovak Republic (14th December 2000). The Commission of the European Communities takes part in the work of the OECD (Article 13 of the OECD Convention).

Publié en français sous le titre :
LES INPÔTS SUR LES COMPAGNIES D'ASSURANCE
N° 3

PREFACE

This study is the third in a series of Tax Policy Studies produced by the Fiscal Affairs Division of the OECD. The series aims to disseminate to a wider audience work undertaken by the OECD Secretariat in the areas of tax policy and tax administration. A list of current and forthcoming studies may be found on the last page.

The current study examines the difficult area of the income taxation of the insurance industry, both life and property and casualty. Particularly in the case of life insurance, OECD countries have pursued a variety of methods to try to tax the income arising in insurance companies. This study analyses the policy and technical problems that arise in designing an effective means of taxation and outlines the approaches that have been taken by a number of OECD countries.

The study begins with an overview of the regulation of the industry, in light of the important linkages between taxation and regulation in this area. It then examines a number of general issues that are faced by all types of insurance companies, (and most financial institutions), noting the need to provide consistent treatment across the different competing segments of this industry, before looking in more detail at the particular issues that arise in the general insurance and life insurance sectors. Finally, a number of alternative ways of taxing these industries are examined.

The purpose of the study is to examine those aspects of an insurer's activities that are intended to be subject to ongoing income taxation. It should be noted that life insurers, and other financial institutions, often play a pivotal role in the provision of private pensions, particularly in Europe. The pension industry is normally subject to a regime of deferred taxation of income. This study does not examine the pension role played by the insurance industry, but concentrates solely on those activities of risk insurance and savings intermediation that are considered to be taxable activities. It should be noted that the dividing line between these types of activities can be difficult to draw and is subject to different approaches in different countries. The study does not attempt to draw conclusions as to where it is appropriate to draw this line other than noting the importance of formulating a clear and consistent policy as to where it should be.

This study has been prepared by David Holland of the OECD Secretariat and Denis Normand of the Department of Finance of Canada. It is based on material that was originally prepared for the Tax Programme for Non-Member Countries. Comments were received from a number of sources including delegates of the Working Party on Tax Analysis and Tax Statistics of the Committee of Fiscal Affairs and the Committee of Insurance. The study is published under the responsibility of the Secretary-General.

INTRODUCTION

Taxation of the insurance industry, particularly the life insurance industry, has long been one of the more problematic areas of income taxation for tax policy makers. The industry has generally developed under a separate regulatory regime from other financial institutions. Its accounting systems are based on complex actuarial computations due to the lags between the assumption of liabilities and payments, and so it is difficult to apply appropriate accrual taxation principles to the calculation of insurance income. As a result the taxation of this industry varies widely across countries and often insurers face a tax regime which is quite different from that applied to other industries in a country.

The unique nature of the industry means that specialised knowledge about its operations is often concentrated in the companies, who place less reliance on outside tax advisors than do many other industries. Accordingly, it can be difficult for a tax policy designer to develop a working knowledge of the income calculations of the industry. And so it can be difficult to design an effective income tax system, particularly for life insurance.

The analysis, which is developed below, examines the issues that arise in trying to tax the insurance industry under income taxation principles. Its point of departure is that the risk management and intermediation functions of the insurance industry should be taxed in a manner which is consistent with that applied to other competing financial intermediaries. It focuses mainly on the taxation of the industry itself and less on the taxation of individual policyholders. In particular the study does not address the important question of the provision of private pensions. Such income is normally subject to a preferential regime of taxation. Life insurers, because of their expertise in managing long-term risks, are often in the forefront of the pension industry.

The paper begins by briefly placing the insurance industry within the context of other financial institutions to provide a framework for judging the appropriate taxation of the industry. In the next section, the nature of the regulation of the industry and its relationship to taxation is explored. A number of general taxation issues, which are common throughout the insurance industry, are then presented. The following sections look in more detail at the specific taxation issues that arise with property and casualty insurance, reinsurance, and life insurance respectively, with a brief reference to issues of policyholder taxation. A number of alternative ways of taxing the industry through non-income taxes are reviewed. The paper concludes with a glossary of technical terms used in the paper. In addition to a policy analysis, each section concludes with a table showing the tax treatment of the industry across a selection of OECD countries.

TABLE OF CONTENTS

Chapter 1. **Insurance as Part of the Financial Industry** 11

The Role of Financial Intermediaries.. 11
Different Institutions... 11
Special Nature of Financial Industry... 12
Competition Among Sectors 12
Treatment of Different Institutions 13
Nature of Insurance 15

Chapter 2. **Regulation of the Financial Institution Industry** 17

Who is to be Regulated? 17
Laws Regulating Activities of Financial Institutions... 17
Areas Commonly Regulated... 18
Constituting the Financial Institution 18
Operations of Financial Institutions.. 18
Dealings with the Public... 19
Making Investments and Market Behaviour 19
Relationship Between Regulation and Tax 20
Conclusion.. 21

Chapter 3. **General Timing and Valuation Issues** 23

Accrual of Income 23
Matching of Revenues and Expenses 23
Issues in Accrual Accounting 24
Bad and Doubtful Debts 27
Reserves 30

Chapter 4. **Issues in International Taxation** 33

Allocating Income and Expenses 33
Reinsurance.. 35
Captive Insurance Companies.. 35
Application of Tax Treaties 36

Chapter 5. **Taxation of Property and Casualty Insurance Companies** 39

Types of P&C Insurance Policies 39
Computation of Insurance Premium 39
Accounting of Income.. 40
Simplified Example.. 40
Cashflow.. 40
Income and Balance Sheet Statements... 41
Comparison of Profit Methods 45
Other Reserves 45
Outstanding Claims Computation 48

Chapter 6. **Comparisons of Selected OECD Countries: Treatment of General Insurance under the Income Tax** 49

Chapter 7. **Taxation and Reinsurance** 53

    Introduction 53
    The Basic Mechanics of Reinsurance 53
    Types of Risks Covered under Reinsurance 53
    Types of Reinsurance Arrangements 54
    Examples of Reinsurance Types 55
    Financial Goals of Reinsurance 56
    Tax Motivations for Reinsurance 58
    Policy Options 59

Chapter 8. **Comparisons of Selected OECD Countries: Treatment of Reinsurance** 63

Chapter 9. **Life Insurance Companies** 65

    Nature of Life Insurance 65
    Types of Insurance Policies 65
    Savings in Life Insurance Policies 66
    Annuities 67
    Company Taxation – Accounting for Income 68
    Policy Reserves 68
    Different Types of Reserves 69
    Impact of Different Reserves on Profit 71
    Immediate Annuities 72
    Mutual Insurers and par Policies 73
    International Taxation Issues 73

Chapter 10. **Comparisons of Selected OECD Countries: Income Taxes on Life Insurers** 77

Chapter 11. **Taxation of Policyholders** 79

    Introduction 79
    Tax Treatment of Premiums Paid by Individuals 79
    Tax Treatment of Benefits Paid to Individuals 80
    Tax Treatment of Employer-paid Premiums 81
    Inside Build up 82
    Methods of Inside Build-up Taxation 83

Chapter 12. **Comparisons of Selected OECD Countries: Policyholder Taxation** 87

Chapter 13. **Alternative Methods of Taxing Financial Institutions** 91

    Issues 91
    Possible Bases 92
    Interaction Between Alternative Tax and Income Tax 93
    Alternative Minimum Taxes 95
    Taxes on Assets or Capital 95
    Premium Taxes 96
    Taxes Based on Reserves 97
    Dividend Relief Systems 97
    Transaction Taxes 97

Chapter 14. **Comparisons of Selected OECD Countries: Premium Taxes on Insurance Companies** 99

Glossary of terms 101

Bibliography 107

List of Boxes

1. Accounting for income (algebraic approach) 72
2. Determining Source of Income and Expenses 74

List of Tables

1. Acceleration of loss 25
2. Asset versus liability adverse selection 26
3. Accounting for reserves 30
4. Discounting 30
5. Foreign companies market share, non-life, 1997 40
6. Cashflow 40
7. Accrual accounting 42
8. Undeferred prepaid expenses 43
9. Reserve for unexpired risks 43
10. Discounting 44
11. Discounting with margins 44
12. Comparison of profit methods 45
13. Outstanding claims computation 46
14. Surplus relief – Non-discounting of outstanding claims 57
15. Loan – Life coinsurance (funds withheld), 40% reinsurance 58
16. Avoiding regulatory restrictions – Life modco (50% basis) 58
17. Transfer of losses – 40% quota share 59
18. Transfer of assets – Life coinsurance (50% quota share) 59
19. Comparison of life insurance reserves 70
20. Impact on profit of life insurance reserves 71
21. Impact of direction of crediting 94

Chapter 1

INSURANCE AS PART OF THE FINANCIAL INDUSTRY

The Role of Financial Intermediaries

Financial intermediaries play a number of important roles in the functioning of a modern market economy. These roles include:

- facilitating the accumulation of savings by individuals by providing a secure place to keep their funds and by offering a return on the capital which is invested;

- intermediation between sources and uses of capital with deposits and investments made by individuals being provided in the form of debt and equity to borrowers;

- diversification of risk through the pooling of funds of different investors so that their capital can be spread over a wide variety of different investments;

- a variety of administrative functions such as record keeping and the evaluation of the credit-worthiness of borrowers and the protection of investors interests in the case of bankruptcy proceeding; and,

- insurance of persons and property to provide private, rather than public, protection from catastrophic events.

In addition to providing insurance, the insurance industry acts as a financial intermediary as insurance companies receive premiums from policyholders and invest the excess of premiums over claims, and so they contribute to the more general benefits from financial intermediation.

Different Institutions

There is no single universally agreed definition of "financial institution". Rather a "financial institution" is one label applied to many diverse bodies. While there are some commonly recognised financial institutions, such as banks and insurance companies, there are others that undertake some of the activities of a "financial institution" without formally being considered to be one.

There are many types of institutions. While they can differ considerably in their apparent form, each plays a part in fulfilling the roles noted above although the emphasis they place on each facet will differ. They will also differ in the types of products that they offer, depending on the financial needs they fill. Examples of financial institutions include:

a) *Deposit-taking institutions*

including banks, savings and loan companies, building societies and trust companies; traditionally they accept deposits and then lend the funds in the form of loans to borrowers;

b) *Property and casualty (P&C) or General insurance*

accept premiums from policyholders for the insurance of risks related to damage or loss of property or third party liabilities;

c) Life insurance

accept premiums from policyholders for the insurance of risks related to loss of health or life or long term disability; as risks may not be realised until far in the future, funds may be invested to fund future risks;

d) Private pension funds

accept contributions from beneficiaries, or as part of a group pension plan, for long term investment in order to fund the payment of pensions after retirement, may be offered by a variety of financial institutions or by specialised pensions funds;

e) Investment funds

accept funds from individuals, which are invested collectively in a variety of debt and equity investments;

f) Leasing companies

offer financing in the form of financial leases, as well as operating leases; and,

g) Financing companies

a variety of institutions, which do not accept deposits directly from the public but offer loans, generally associated with consumer purchases; they are often subsidiaries of manufacturing companies which aid in the financing of its products.

Special Nature of Financial Industry

The ordinary rules in the income tax are not well adapted for the financial industry. The industry will often be subject to special accounting regimes which may be developed under the authority of the regulator and which may differ from normal accounting rules, *e.g.* by allowing/requiring the marking to market of certain assets and liabilities. The industry has special products such as insurance policies, which require precise mathematical specification. Accordingly, the industry will often have separate rules in the tax system. For example a general allowance for bad debts may be allowed without the requirement, which applies to ordinary businesses, that the amounts previously have been included in income. Deductions for certain types of contingent liabilities, such as for risks arising as part of an insurance contract, may be allowed before the liability to payment has become fixed and determinable, unlike for ordinary taxpayers.

Competition Among Sectors

In the past, the different sectors had developed in distinct fashions, generally under different regulatory and accounting regimes. Accordingly, the taxation regimes often included substantial differences in treatment across the industries of what were economically similar transactions. However more recently there has been a blurring of these distinctions among industries. Their products increasingly are substitutes. Certain life insurance policies, or their close relatives, annuities, compete directly with certificates of deposit offered by banks in the market for long-term savings, particularly for retirement. Increasing inter-sectoral ownership, often in response to a relaxation of previous rules enforced by regulators that prohibited cross-ownership, means that different institutions can now offer or market directly competing products. Finally, the traditional distinction between credit and other forms of risk is blurring with insurance companies beginning to insure particular risks, (such as crop failure or exchange movements) as part of financing deals. In such circumstances it is important that the tax system treats what are economically equivalent transactions the same. Unfortunately, most traditional tax systems, as applied to the insurance industry in particular, fail this test.

Treatment of Different Institutions

It is instructive to make a comparison of how the two principal financial industries, deposit-taking institutions and life insurance companies operate and are taxed. The basic situation described is that of the standard income taxation of financial income. In many countries special rules that will diverge from the paradigm described below apply to certain types of savings vehicles. The important point to recognise is that, in principle, while the calculation of income is substantially different for deposit-taking institutions and insurance companies, the two methods can be made equivalent if properly constructed.

Deposit-taking institutions receive deposits of principal from the depositor and make investments with these funds, on which they earn interest. They pay interest to the depositor while the deposit is outstanding and eventually return the principal to the depositor, generally at the maturity of the contract, which may be fixed or on demand.

Insurance companies receive premiums from policyholders. They make investments with premiums and eventually make a payment of insurance proceeds to the policyholder on receiving a claim, termination or in some cases on maturation of the policy. There may be a substantial difference in the time of receipt of the premium and the payments of any claims on the policy. The premium partly pays for the insurance for risk and partly contains a savings component. For the life industry, the savings component may be large. In some cases the product may be sold primarily as a savings vehicle, with a return of investment at maturity even if no claims are made under the risk portion of the contract. For P&C insurers, the savings element is small for most products (which generally are for one year only) and so the product is rarely sold as a savings vehicle.

1. Tax Treatment of Amounts – Deposit-taking Institutions

a) Institution

The principal received from (returned to) the depositor is not taxable (deductible), as an equal and opposite liability is established (extinguished) as the asset is received (returned) and so no net income results from the transaction. The income earned on the investments made with the funds is taxable in the hands of the institution and the interest paid to, or accrued on behalf of, depositors is deductible in calculating the income of the institution.

b) Investor

Similarly, the principal is neither deductible nor taxable in the hands of the depositor and the interest that is received, or accrued, is taxable.

2. Tax Treatment of Amounts – Life Insurance Companies

a) Institution

The entire premium received is taxable to the company. Any investment income that is earned on the funds is taxable. When payments for claims are due and payable they are deductible – including both the amounts which correspond to interest earned on behalf of the policyholder and the return of principal. In order to avoid significant upfront taxation of the premium that is received, a reserve provision is allowed for the future liability of the company implicit in the contract. The calculation of the reserve generally implies that an interest expense with respect to the policy is deductible as it accrues. The crucial problem, which leads to this different form of taxation, is to distinguish between the portion of the premium which is a purchase of protection from risk (an act of consumption) and the portion which is in effect a payment of principal for the savings component inherent in the premium. (This description only covers countries that seek to separate the income accruing to the company from the income accruing to the policyholder. I-E systems, which tax the entire investment income accruing on the policy, are described elsewhere in the report.)

b) Business policyholder

For businesses the purchase of insurance (at least property and term life insurance) is a legitimate business expense and so the premium is deductible. Accordingly, any payment that is received should be taxable. For certain types of policies there may be a significant delay between the payment and deduction of the premium and the receipt and taxation of the benefits. This mismatch of timing gives rise to the possibility of a deferral of tax, unless accrued interest on the policy is taxed which it generally is not.

c) Individual policyholder

Under an income tax the premiums paid by individual policyholders on life insurance should neither be deductible (being a combination of consumption of insurance protection and a deposit of principal, and not an expense to earn income) nor should the pure insurance proceeds be taxable as they simply compensate for a loss which has occurred. In fact the treatment of premiums paid by individuals varies widely among countries. Any interest accruing with respect to the policy should be taxed as it accrues on behalf of the individual policyholder, (assuming that ordinary interest is taxed as it accrues). Again treatment varies widely across countries. In many instances there is no taxation of accrued interest; in some countries, it is implicitly taxed at the company level; and in others it is taxed at cash surrender or possibly on the receipt of a claim. Annuity products tend to be treated under the regime applied to interest-bearing instruments.

3. Substitution of Instruments

Life insurance policies can be designed so that savings, rather than insurance, is the primary motivation for the purchase of the policy. Generally, if much of the premium is returned through certain payments, which may occur at a fixed date or on demand if there is not a death claim on the policy, then the policy is more of a savings vehicle than an insurance policy. Much of the premium, which is paid today, is returned in the future in a manner similar to the return of principal to a depositor. The policyholder receives some compensation for the time value of money, which is an implicit interest return. Without special rules this interest may escape taxation. Other products offered by the life insurance industry, such as fixed term annuities, are direct substitutes for deposits. Deferred annuities are a bundling of deposit and insurance components. Even in the P&C insurance industry, where most contracts are of short-duration, deferred or structured settlements have an implicit saving component. Accordingly, rather than being distinct instruments when compared to deposits, insurance policies form a continuum which at one end has close substitutes to deposits and other forms of savings.

4. Separating Income of Investor and Company

The challenge in designing the tax system for life insurance is to split the return which is made on the deposit/premium between that which is earned by the company and that which is earned by the individual. (I-E systems seek to avoid this by taxing the entire investment return at the company level.) For deposit-taking institutions, the accounting is simpler since an explicit interest amount is generally credited to the depositor and can be deducted by the institution and taxed as income in the depositor's hands. However in the case of insurance, part of the premium is a contribution of principal to be returned to the policyholder and part is a payment for insurance. Interest accrues over the life of the policy and part of insurance proceeds is a return of interest that has accrued over the life of the policy. That interest has been implicitly deducted by the company as it accrued through the operation of the policy reserve and so can be considered to have been earned on behalf of the policyholder. To have a parallel treatment with interest earned on deposits and bonds, it should be taxed as it accrues.

Nature of Insurance

Contracts of insurance *pool risks* among many risk averse persons[1] through the payment of an amount (called a premium) to be indemnified against the risk of financial loss. The premium is usually a small amount compared to the amount that is possibly lost under an insured event. For example, for a small premium a business owner can insure its warehouse against fire, theft and other property risks. If one of these events occurs and the insured did not provide false information on the contract and the accident was a random occurrence or Act of God, the insured is indemnified for an amount of its losses. Insurance contracts typically have a coinsurance clause where the insured shares some portion of the loss.

The *pooling of risks* that insurers perform is a form of financial intermediation – that is, the insurer acts to collect funds from persons wishing to insure themselves against certain risks. The pricing of the premiums must take into account the expected losses of the "pool of insureds" over the term of the insurance contract. This computation is made more predictable with historic data as there are a large number of insureds – that is; the *law of large numbers* applies. As premiums are usually collected in advance of payments for claims, the funds are invested by the insurer to earn a return, *i.e.* a form of financial intermediation, even if the policyholder does not explicitly have an investment motive. The investment return will be included in the insurer's computation of the appropriate level of premium.

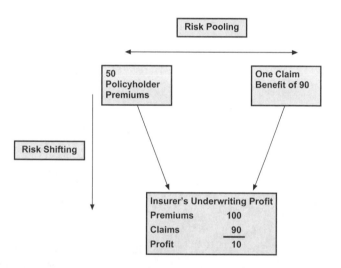

Risks are shifted to the insurer to the extent that the insurer cannot adjust premiums in an *ad hoc* manner to compensate for losses. The result from the insurer's perspective is that it assumes an *underwriting risk* equal to the amount by which claims and expenses could exceed premiums. Insured persons are able to transfer risks to the insurer and ultimately to current or future policyholders and/or shareholders of the insurance company.

To the extent that an insurer assumes underwriting risks (that is, it is unable to pass on the underwriting risks to current and future policyholders), it will command a risk premium that will compensate shareholders for the risks they are assuming. Thus for an insurer that takes on very risky forms of insurance, the return required by the insurer will be higher than for less risky forms of insurance.

The insurance industry is generally broken into two segments. Property and casualty insurance (P&C or general insurance) and life insurance. In fact, many countries do not allow insurers to sell both

---

1. Risk neutral or risk loving persons will choose not to insure.

property and casualty and life insurance business in the same corporate entity due to the difference in the nature of risks assumed by the insurer. P&C insurers generally insure the risk of financial loss arising from damage or loss of property through fire, theft or third party liability. Life insurers concentrate on replacing financial loss due to death or sickness of individuals. While each industry has particular issues with their taxation, they do share a number of concepts in common. These issues are explored in the Chapter on the general issues in taxation.

Insurance intermediation is performed by stock insurers (those with share capital), mutual insurers (no share capital, policyholders are effectively the owners), co-operatives (such as farmer co-operatives), and fraternal benefit societies (which may be created by athletic associations, religious or ethnic groups).

Chapter 2

REGULATION OF THE FINANCIAL INSTITUTION INDUSTRY[1]

Who is to be Regulated?

As noted above there is no simple definition of what constitutes a financial institution and the term can be considered to cover both the formal financial institutions and others that are more informal. For regulators, the question is to determine what are the most important characteristics of what will be formal, and therefore regulated, financial institutions.

There are two main activities in financial intermediation which would generally be considered to be part of the work of a financial institution. These are receiving funds from the public and then passing them on in some form to those who would use those funds. For the most part, regulators are most concerned with the acceptance of funds, be they in the form of deposits in banks, or premiums for insurance policies. Their concern is with the solvency of the institution for the protection of the depositor/policyholder/investor. Therefore regulators will target those institutions which accept funds from the public.

For taxation authorities, this distinction may not in itself be sufficient when there are special tax rules for financial institutions, for example to determine the ability to claim reserves for bad debts against income or in the computation of interest or in the application of a VAT. In such cases a more general definition may be necessary. In other words, not all companies, which are considered to be financial institutions for taxation purposes, will be subject to financial regulation.

Nevertheless, there are a number of types of institutions that are generally recognised to be financial institutions and will be subject to strict regulation. These include: insurance companies – life and property and casualty insurers; banks and other deposit-taking bodies – savings and loans or credit unions; pension funds; investment funds; and securities dealers.

Others, such as leasing companies, dealers in factors/derivatives/currency, consumer finance operations of retailers and finance conduit companies in corporate groups, will have some aspects of financial activity and so may be subject to certain financial regulations. These may be contained in general laws for which there may not be a specific regulatory authority.

Laws Regulating Activities of Financial Institutions

The consequence of this diversity of companies with a financial component to their businesses is that the regulation of these bodies is covered in many different laws. Some of these laws are specific to the institution being regulated and comprehensively cover most aspects of regulation. Others are more general, applying to non-financial corporations as well and may cover many different areas. Examples include:

- corporations law (for all corporations)
- banking laws
- insurance company laws

---

1. This section is substantially based on a presentation prepared by Graeme Cooper for the OECD's Tax Programme for non-Member Countries.

- investment fund/social security laws
- securities and commodity dealers regulations
- stock/futures/commodity exchange regulations
- consumer credit laws (if giving credit to customers)
- consumer protection laws (if offering loans or investments to the public)

Areas Commonly Regulated

In general, the government will wish to regulate four aspects of financial institutions operations. These are:

- constituting the financial institution;
- daily operation of the financial institution;
- dealings with the public; and,
- behaviour of the financial institution when making investments with invested funds.

It is important that the regulatory regime be strong in order to ensure investor confidence. This is the basis of the intermediation function and is necessary so that capital markets can be formed to act as a bridge between diverse savers and large borrowers

Constituting the Financial Institution

A number of laws may be concerned with the establishment of the institution. Some, such as those concerning the legal form, will be of general application. Others will be specific to the type of financial institution in question, particularly when the institution is subject to a special regulatory regime. Taken as a whole the laws will contain provisions covering a variety of issues.

The institution will typically be in the form of a separate legal person, which implies that it has its own name, has the ability to sue and be sued and has a perpetual life. Provisions will also be included which divide the rights to profits and assets among owners, investors and creditors. In many cases for deposit-taking institutions, the form of the institution will be as a corporation or joint stock company. However for other institutions some other form may be possible and even normal. Other possibilities include trusts, mutual companies or co-operatives.

Separate laws will cover different aspects of the institution, reflecting particular policy objectives. For example, there may be a requirement for a minimum amount of invested capital by shareholders, as a means of protecting depositors/policyholder/investors by ensuring that there is sufficient economic and financial substance to the enterprise. Other rules may limit the extent of foreign ownership that is allowed or may restrict the percentage holding of any particular shareholder, to ensure that the companies are widely-held.

Operations of Financial Institutions

The regulatory laws will also contain provisions about the conduct of managers with respect to their appointment and removal and their responsibilities and powers. The laws will have restrictions on managers dealing with the institution in order to avoid conflict of interest situations where the manager could make an undue profit from transactions with the corporation over which he could have influence or control. Managers will also be prohibited from engaging in insider trading whereby they profit from knowledge gained as part of their duties.

The law will also outline the required accounts and reports. For regulated financial institutions this will usually be contained in their special regulatory law. It will list the prescribed information to be reported, the form and content for preparing accounts and often the major accounting methodology to be employed. These accounts may in some instances depart from the standard accounting rules followed by ordinary corporations. It is in the area of accounting that the greatest overlaps between taxation rules and regulatory rules occur. On the other hand, some accounting concepts which are appropriate for regulatory purposes may not be appropriate for tax purposes and so adjustments to the accounts prepared for the regulator will be necessary.

Dealings with the Public

Regulatory and consumer protection laws will contain rules designed to ensure that consumers are fully informed about the nature of their financial transactions. The law will contain rules about the manner of soliciting for depositors and investors. Extensive information will be required so that investors can analyse the financial consequences of their decisions. Interest rates will need to be reported on a standard basis to facilitate comparison. For other types of investments, it will be necessary to make profit projections and disclose financial information relevant to the potential for gain and loss of the investment.

The supporting documentation should also reveal the management fees and profits of the promoters and the nature of the investor's interest in the institution, the investors' ability to trade in interests and the power of the institution to redeem an interest. Finally, reports will be required to disclose the results of the investment to the investor.

Making Investments and Market Behaviour

Many of the most important rules involve what forms of business the institution may be involved in and rules that are designed to protect the funds of depositors and policyholders.

1. Types of activities

One set of rules will determine what types of activities a particular institution may be engaged in. There may be rules prohibiting certain kinds of investments or carrying on certain kinds of businesses. For example banks may be prohibited from selling insurance. In many countries there has been a tradition of separating the pillars of the financial intermediation industry – deposit-taking institutions, insurance and securities dealing. One motivation for this was to insulate the different sectors from solvency shocks in other sectors – *i.e.* to prevent the spread of weakness in the insurance sector into the banking sector. It also made the job of regulators easier as they could concentrate only on certain types of systemic risk. On the other hand it also insulated existing firms in the market segments from direct competition from other sectors (a major factor no doubt in the reluctance of some sectors to see the fall of the three pillar concept). And it may have increased risk by reducing the ability of firms to diversify across a broad range of financial products.

The reality is however that financial products in different sub-sectors do compete. And this competition has become more explicit as institutions have found ways to tailor their products to provide the types of benefits more traditionally found in the products of other institutions. For example, life insurers have traditionally provided annuities. With a life annuity or deferred annuity there is a strong insurance component as the amount of payment is a function of the life expectancy of the annuitant. However defined period annuities, which may be transferable on death to the beneficiaries, function economically like a certificate of deposit in a bank, even if the legal form is different.

Accordingly, in many jurisdictions the old regulatory distinction among the different pillars is breaking down. The change recognises economic reality and is intended to promote competition and more efficient financial arrangements.

2. Solvency regulations

At the heart of the regulatory regime for any financial institution are the solvency regulations. It is this aspect of government oversight that is fundamental to providing depositors and investors with confidence in the integrity of their financial institutions. This confidence, in turn, is fundamental to securing the funds from depositors that are needed to start the financial intermediation process. The Great Depression and recent events in Asia have underlined the extent to which a fall in confidence in the banking sector of a country can have a substantial damaging impact on real activity through a collapse of the availability of credit.

Accordingly stringent, and increasingly sophisticated measures, are applied to ensure that financial institutions have sufficient capital and reserves to withstand adverse shocks on the financial system, such as an abnormally high number of defaults in the case of banks or a large natural disaster in the case of insurance. These rules may be buttressed by additional restrictions, for example requiring minimum deposits with government or investments in government securities or restrictions on borrowing to reduce the potential claims on the assets of the institution in the face of bankruptcy. The solvency rules are an important cornerstone of financial regulation and their requirements will heavily influence the nature of the accounts required by regulators. In some cases this will imply an emphasis on the balance sheet rather than the income statement and so concepts may be developed which are less appropriate for taxation purposes.

3. *Prudential investment practices*

For some institutions, such as pension funds and mutual funds, the restrictions may be less in the form of capital adequacy ratios and may be targeted at ensuring a "prudent" investment policy is followed. Such restrictions may be in the form of maximum percentages of a portfolio in a single investment, a maximum percentage interest allowed in a single company or the necessity that the firm being invested in has maintained a history of dividend payments.

Relationship Between Regulation and Tax

The taxation and regulatory regimes share a similar objective in that they seek to measure the economic well-being and strength of financial institutions: the former in order to determine the taxation capacity of the institution; the latter in order to ensure that the institution remains financially healthy. Accordingly, they cover many of the same issues, particularly in the area of accounting. If the regulatory regime is well designed and well administered, then it should be possible to rely upon the regulatory regime for **some** tax purposes as well. The regulatory regime will often have a special accounting system more appropriate for the industry than the general accounting rules. Financial institution regulators will generally have specialised skills and knowledge about industry, for example in evaluating the degree of bad or doubtful debts. This can be particularly important in countries, which are just developing financial sophistication, both within and without the government, where there will likely be a shortage of skilled financial analysts.

But the principal objective of financial institution industry regulators is safeguarding investor's funds and ensuring that the balance sheet of the institution is sound. This is achieved by controlling the level of risk undertaken by financial institutions, requiring financial institutions to disclose their activities and performance in a standard form and maintaining minimum capital requirements for financial institutions. This objective is seen in rules about risk-weighting of investments, capital adequacy ratios, conservative valuation of assets, special reserves for future liabilities and computing profits that can be returned to investors. The income in the year is not a critical issue and in fact the regulator may prefer rules which allow a smoothing of income fluctuations over the business cycle.

In contrast, the principal objective of tax system is to collect the revenue that is properly owed, based upon the current year's profit. In pursuing this objective in a manner that minimises tax avoidance, the tax authorities prefer precise rules that do not depend upon estimates.

Therefore the goals of regulators and tax system do not always coincide and the provisions in the two systems may differ in significant ways. While both systems try to be accurate, the regulatory rules are intended to ensure that profits and therefore capital are not over-estimated, while tax authorities are concerned with the opposite tendency to minimise reported income.

Differences between the two goals will be seen in:

- regulatory rules which are focused on the accurate computation of net capital, not net income (*i.e.* the use of special baskets of assets to determine which assets will be allocated to a jurisdiction for regulatory purposes differ fundamentally from source rules use to allocate taxable revenue);

- regulatory rules for computing profit which require conservative valuation of assets (*i.e.* lower of cost or market) and special reserves for future liabilities (*i.e.* general contingent reserves or income smoothing accounts); the corresponding tax rules could be mark-to market for assets and the denial of a deduction for contingent reserves; and,

- the form and content of accounts and reports will differ because the items that are considered critical are different depending upon the questions that are focused on at audit stage.

A further problem is that many important tax questions will not be explicitly addressed in regulatory laws, as they are not critical to its operation and objectives. For example, is the institution a separate taxpayer or is it simply a flow-through vehicle? What is the precise legal form of the investment made by the depositor/ policyholder/ investor? Is it a bank deposit, insurance policy or mutual fund? How are special reserves required by regulations treated for tax purposes? Capital adequacy rules may allow (insist on) special kinds of debt interests as part of capital *i.e.* subordinated debt and permanent debt. These may be treated as capital for regulatory purposes but give rise to tax deductible interest payments rather than dividends. What is the jurisdictional source of income and how are expenses to be allocated across jurisdictions? Regulators may be more concerned with ensuring that there are enough assets to cover future claims arising within their jurisdiction, rather than the allocation of each type of the income to the different jurisdictions.

Accordingly the exact relationship between the tax and regulatory rules must be carefully examined and specified in detail. Clearly the establishment of a sound financial sector, a cornerstone of which is rigorous regulation, is a fundamental goal of economic policy and an important condition for sustained economic growth. While the tax system should not jeopardise this goal, it is not necessary for the tax system to adopt all aspects of the rules and deductions mandated under the regulatory regime.

The tax system rules can help to promote critical parts of the regulatory accounting regime. For example, a reasonable provision should be made for the deduction of expenses. Including a deduction for specific bad debts, which have been reported to the regulator, increases the incentive for the institution to comply with the regulatory authority. On the other hand allowing deductions for general reserves, based on formulae, provides tax benefits when there may not be a cost to the institution without increasing an incentive toward better disclosure.

In conclusion, there will be permanent differences between the regulatory accounts and the tax accounts. Tax rules can be based in part on regulatory accounts but with special entries reversed, the profit computations will need to be largely reconstructed and there must be explicit rules about some special factors. In determining the extent of the differences that should be allowed, a number of considerations are important. First, the tax authorities, particularly in the early years of establishing financial markets may lack experience with the complicated transactions found in the financial world. To the extent that this expertise resides with the regulators, the tax administration may wish to rely as much as possible on the audits performed by the regulators. In this case, differences would arise from the denial of specific categories of reserves, for example, rather than an independent valuation of the potential for loan loss by the tax inspector. The second consideration is the compliance burden imposed on the institutions in order to maintain two separate sets of accounts. To the extent that entries can be the same, this burden is reduced.

Conclusion

The regulatory regimes directed at the financial sector play an important role in establishing a sound and effective financial sector. On the other hand, the tax regimes are essential in preserving government revenues. Both cover many of the same aspects of the economic behaviour of the financial sector. While where possible consistency should be maintained between the two to reduce compliance and administrative burden, some differences are inevitable, given the differing objectives of the two systems.

Chapter 3

GENERAL TIMING AND VALUATION ISSUES

Insurance companies, like other financial institutions, face a variety of issues related to the timing of recognition of income and expenses. Many of the most complex issues associated with the measurement of the income of insurance companies arise with the timing of income and expenses. Companies naturally seek to advance the recognition of expenses and to defer the recognition of revenue in order to reduce their effective rate of taxation.

Accounting has traditionally tried to deal with these issues through the use of accrual taxation and the matching principle. More recently valuation systems such as mark-to-market have been introduced to try to eliminate the timing issues which have arisen with accrual accounting. The tax system has had to adopt these and other technical rules in an attempt to prevent undue timing advantages to be gained through the structuring of transactions.

Accrual of Income

In the absence of other over-riding policy considerations, the goal of an income tax should be to tax the economic income associated with an enterprise. This would generally comply with the goals of taxation of fairness – taxing income at the same rate regardless of its source, and neutrality – not distorting the allocation of economic activity. From an accounting for income point of view, this principle has its basic expression in the **accrual principle**, which seeks to recognise income as it arises, rather than waiting for an actual payment to be made.

Under accrual taxation principles, which apply to the calculation of income from most businesses, revenues and expenses are accounted for as they are earned or incurred. In its purest form, this would imply that all assets and liabilities would need to be valued each year to recognise any gain or loss which had occurred during that year. This would impose a significant compliance burden and would require a subjective estimation of value in cases where no direct market price exists for a particular asset. Therefore in most cases the **realisation principle** is applied. In general, an event where the asset or liability becomes fixed and determinable, such as a sale, must occur to trigger the recognition of the amount as revenue or an expense.

However, in some instances, deviations from a pure accrual principle are necessary, either to achieve certain policy goals or to facilitate compliance with the tax. In these situations circumstances could arise where the revenues and their associated costs are accounted for with different timing. To avoid this, the **matching principle** is also often applied. In this case an attempt is made to have the expenses associated with revenues recognised at the same time.

While, in general, insurance companies account for their income according to the accrual principle of accounting, there are a number of significant differences in how the accrual rules are applied to the industry as compared to other industries. These arise from the particular nature of the industry and the need to be more precise in the specification of the income arising on financial products given their importance in determining income.

Matching of Revenues and Expenses

If expenses can be recognised before the associated income is taxed, a deferral of tax occurs. If on the other hand, income is recognised without making adequate allowance for related expenses, too much tax will be paid, or it will be paid too soon. The insurance industry, which in many cases incurs obligations to make payments that will not occur until far in the future faces both of these issues to a significant degree. Accordingly, many special rules have been developed to achieve a better matching of income and expenses than would occur with a simple application of the principles which are generally applied in other industries.

In some cases, expenses, such as acquisition and commission expenses, are incurred before the premium and investment income associated with the policy are included in income. In order to avoid a deferral of taxation through the deduction of these expenses before the income is recognised, special reserving techniques are available in both the P&C and life insurance industries, although they are not universally employed for either accounting or tax purposes among OECD countries.

In other cases, income is received in the form of premiums which will not be taxed in the current year. This may occur because the policy straddles a year end, so that some of the risks which are being insured will not expire until the next year. Or in may result from the fact that the policy covers many years and the current premium may not related only to this year's risks. Again, the industry uses the mechanisms of reserves to achieve a better matching of income and expenses. Questions arise as to which future expenses and in what amount should be recognised when. In particular, should such expenses be discounted to achieve a better matching in terms as value as well as time?

Issues in Accrual Accounting

A number of particular issues arise with the application of the accrual principle to interest-bearing and other securities. Since insurance companies typically have a large portfolio of bonds and similar investments, these problems are particularly acute for them.

1. Accrual of Interest

While many ordinary taxpayers report interest on a receivable basis (*i.e.* the date at which a payment is due on the instrument), financial institutions typically use a pure accrual basis. Interest is calculated on a daily basis, and then assigned to the taxation year in which it has accrued. Some instruments are issued at a discount (an original issue discount, OID), where the price paid for the bond at issue is less than the principal that will be returned at maturity. The discount yields an implicit yield to maturity depending upon the term to maturity. The yield to maturity reflects a market interest rate. Discounted instruments can also be created by "stripping" bonds; that is, separating the stream of interest payments from the repayment of principal at maturity. In effect two instruments, a level payment annuity and a discount bond are created.

Without special rules, the discount may be treated as a capital gain on maturity or sale, which is taxed only at maturity and perhaps at preferential tax rates applying to capital gains. To avoid this, most countries accrue the discount as "interest" income which is allocated to the tax years in which it is accumulated, on a compound yield to maturity basis.

2. Problems with Realisation Taxation

Discounts (and premiums) can also occur as a result of movements in the market rate of interest after a fixed interest rate bond has been issued, whenever the coupon interest rate (if any) on a security traded in the secondary market is below (or above) market interest rates.

For example, a discount bond paying 100 in one year's time has a value of:

- 91 if the market interest rate is 10% ($100 \div 1.10$)
- 87 if the market interest rate is 15% ($100 \div 1.15$)

So if interest rates go up (down), bond prices go down (up)

For ordinary taxpayers, the fall in the price of the bond is treated as a capital loss on realisation (*i.e.*, the sale of the bond). This can give rise to problems with both the timing of taxation and the characterisation of income.

If gains and losses of bonds are treated as capital gains and if capital gains are taxed preferentially relative to ordinary income, then the firm can deduct its costs of borrowing against fully-taxed income (*i.e.* through the reserve calculations), but have part of its revenues taxed at preferential rates. Given the thin margins in the intermediation businesses, this advantage can substantially reduce taxable income. One policy response is to treat all income on financial assets of financial institutions as income, rather than as a capital gain. Income treatment is appropriate on the basis that the trading of investment assets is part of the ordinary business of the company and the gains and losses arising on the purchase of investment assets are an integral part of the expected return.

However, even if the gains and losses are treated as income, realisation taxation gives rise to four timing problems:

a) Deferred recognition of income

When assets are purchased at a market discount, the total yield to be earned from the bond is the coupon rate of interest plus the yield to maturity rate of return on the difference between the purchase price and the face value of the bond at maturity. On the other hand the financing costs with respect to the funds invested are implicitly deductible as part of the policy reserve calculation. Therefore, there is a timing mismatch between the deferred recognition of the income arising from the discount (recognised at maturity) and the immediate deduction of the related costs.

b) Acceleration of Loss

As interest rates fluctuate, financial assets will go up and down in value. A timing advantage can be gained by selling an asset that has declined in value and replacing it with another that is substantially similar. The result is a deferral of tax: deduct the loss now and accrue higher income over the remaining term of the replacement asset.

Example:

1. Bond #1 acquired Jan 1 1999 for 83 (interest rate 10%). Face value of 100 at maturity Dec. 31 2000. Discount of 17 accrued over 2 tax years

2. Bond #1 sold Dec. 31 1999 when the market interest rate has risen to 15%. Loss on sale is the market value at Dec. 31 1999 of 87 = (100 ÷ 1.15) minus the amortised cost of 91 (83 of cost plus 8 of accrued interest that has been already subject to tax) for a loss of 4.

3. Bond #2 acquired Jan 1 2000 for 87, maturing Dec. 31 2000. Discount of 13 (100-87) accrued as interest in 2000.

The following table compares the tax results of holding Bond #1 to maturity and the case where it is sold at the end of 1999 and replaced by a Bond #2, with the same date of maturity. Overall the total income that is taxed is the same, 17, but in the latter case some of the income is deferred until the second year. If interest rates continue a steady decline over a period of years, the effective deferral period from selling discounted bonds can be substantial.

Table 1. **Acceleration of loss**

		1999	2000
	No sale		
1	Accrual of interest	8	9
	Sale and repurchase		
2	Accrual of interest on bond #1	8	
3	Loss on sale of bond #1	4	
4	Accrual of interest on bond #2	..	*13*
5	Profit **(2 – 3 + 4)**	4	13

c) Asset Versus Liability Adverse Selection

An insurance company tries to match its assets and liabilities in order to insulate itself from fluctuations in, for example, interest rates and exchange rates by ensuring that both sides of its portfolio move in concert. If interest rates go up, it can sell its assets at a loss and buy an asset with a higher yield as with the acceleration of loss example. This can lead to an artificial loss as the associated liability has also declined in value, but the loss is not recognised. This is a general problem for financial institutions. In the case of insurance companies, most of the liabilities are in the form of reserves. If these reserves are computed at the implicit rate of interest at the time of entering into the insurance contract, and if there is no corresponding adjustment of value, then they will be able to take advantage of such adverse selection in periods of increasing, or fluctuating, interest rates. In order to avoid this problem it is necessary to revalue annually such liabilities at current interest rates, (see section on Mark to Market).

Example:

1. Jan. 1 1999: Insurance company issues a 2-year insurance contract and receives a premium of 83. Contract matures on Dec. 31 2000 with a cash surrender value of 100 (market interest rate of 10 per cent). Policy reserve of 83 established at issue, reserve increases at rate of interest of 10 per cent, *i.e.* 8 in 1999 and 9 in 2000.

2. Jan. 1 1999: Insurance company uses the funds from the premium to buy Bond #1 for 83 maturing on Dec. 31 2000, face value of 100, matching its assets to its liabilities.

3. Dec. 31 1999: The market interest rate rises to 15 per cent. Bond #1 is sold for 87. Bond #2 is acquired for 87, maturing on Dec. 31 2000 for 100.

Table 2. **Asset versus liability adverse selection**

		1999	2000
	Scenario 1 (no sale)		
1	Premium received/Reversal of reserve[1]	83	100
2	Accrual of interest on bond #1	8	9
3	Establishment of reserve/Payment of claim	83	100
4	Accumulation of Reserve	8	9
	Profit **(1 + 2) – (3 + 4)**	0	0
	Scenario 2 (sale of Bond #1/acquire Bond #2)		
1	Accrual of interest on bond #1	8	
2	Loss on sale of bond #1	4	
3	Accrual of interest on bond #2		13
4	Net Expense of policy reserve **3 + 4 – 1**	8	9
	Profit (with sale) **1 – 2 + 3 – 4**	–4	4

1. See section on Reserves below for mechanics of reserve accounting.

d) Assets Versus Asset Adverse Selection

Insurance companies hold large portfolios of equity investments. They can "adverse select" among such assets under a realisation basis of taxation. In this case, companies continue to hold shares that have accumulated unrealised gains and sell shares that are in a loss. Thus taxation is deferred on the unrealised gains, but the losses are deducted immediately. In situations where countries use a "lower of cost or market value" inventory accounting for financial assets, this result is achieved automatically.

A variety of rules are employed to minimise this possibility. If the trading of equity is considered to give rise to a capital gain, then it is typical to allow capital losses to be deductible only against capital gains that have been realised on other assets. However, if the sale were treated as giving rise to ordinary income, then typically there would be no restriction. A loss may be denied for artificial "wash sales", where the asset sold is replaced by another asset which is substantially the same within a fixed period, (say 30 days after or *before* the sale).

3. Mark to market or Fair Value

While specific anti-avoidance measures exist for some of the problems noted above, others are inherent in the system of realisation taxation. Accordingly a number of countries have sought a more comprehensive solution to the problems. The approach, which has been adopted, is to apply a "mark-to market" principle. Under mark to market, a market valuation is made of the net value of all financial assets and liabilities at the end of the year. These amounts are then compared to their values at the beginning of the year to determine the gain or loss on the instruments.

Market valuation of all assets *and liabilities* eliminates adverse selection as both losses and gains are recorded as they occur. For example, asset to asset adverse selection is eliminated as both gains and losses are recognised as they occur, so that it is not possible to defer the recognition of gains while recognising losses. Asset to liability adverse selection is similarly eliminated when liabilities are also marked to market. As assets and liabilities are in principle matched in term and characteristics by financial institutions, the amounts recognised should generally be offsetting. Acceleration of losses however is not prevented to the extent that there is a net assets position, not offset by liabilities subject to mark to market. In fact, one effect of mark to market is to recognise losses immediately, reducing income to the extent that the losses have not been hedged by a gain on the corresponding liability. However, unhedged gains can no longer be deferred, and are now taxed as they occur and so over time the two effects will balance.

Mark to market implies that all (financial) assets and liabilities need to be valued. Valuation is certainly complex, with millions of assets and liabilities for large financial institutions. In some cases, determining market value may be difficult. Appropriate valuations may not exist for thinly traded assets (illiquid markets). Questions arise as to which values to use, bid, ask or midpoint price, the treatment of future administration charges (deduct from market value which requires subjective estimation) and treatment of creditworthiness – increased risk may be reflected in the market value, but the recognition of the valuation may not be consistent with loan loss provisions allowed for taxation purposes. However by their nature, many assets are tradable and for those which are not, standard techniques exist for valuation and are employed in the financial institutions own portfolio management. Moreover, standard accounting for the insurance industry is moving towards mark to market. In general, sophisticated insurance companies have the capacity for the calculation.

A particular problem for insurance companies is that the bulk of their liabilities are contained in their reserves. In principle, the value of reserves should reflect the discounting of future liabilities. However, in many countries, P&C insurance companies do not use discounting in calculating claims reserves. And life companies, which do discount, may not revalue reserves as market interest rates change. In such cases a number of the mismatching problems noted above may occur, since the offsetting gain or loss on the liabilities is not accounted for as the loss or gain on the assets is registered.

Another concern is that mark to market can cause uneven patterns of income and losses, as market values fluctuate. This can certainly occur for inherently volatile assets such as stocks. In this case, tax may be paid before the sale of the assets, potentially causing cash flow problems. For most taxpayers, this is one of the principal arguments for realisation taxation. But financial institutions have the capacity for self-financing. Furthermore, for many assets, the corresponding liabilities are matched and so the net impact is greatly reduced. Even if swings do occur, loss carry-overs can smooth large swings.

Bad and Doubtful Debts

Insurance companies like other financial institutions make loans and purchase bonds issued by governments and corporations. Some portion of these instruments will suffer from a full or partial default, that is they give rise to a bad debt.

For most taxpayers, bad debts may only be recognised to the extent that an amount has previously been included in income. This is a necessary consequence of accrual taxation, which recognises income as it accrues, before payment is made. If it is eventually determined that payment will not be received then it is appropriate that the previous income inclusion be reversed. Losses on other loans, on the other hand would be treated as capital in nature. However for financial institutions, *i.e.* those companies which are in the business of lending money, it is appropriate to relax this restriction and allow bad debts on the lending assets of the institution to be deducted from income even if they represent the principal of a loan, rather than the reversal of an amount that has previously been accrued into income. The reason for this is that the interest income of a financial institution includes a risk premium which is intended to compensate for the possibility of default on the loan. Therefore, the deduction of the bad debt offsets this income inclusion.

The timing of the deduction is also an issue. A number of countries, the United States and Australia for example, require that a debt be bad before a deduction is allowed. No deduction is allowed for doubtful debts, so the recognition of loan losses is deferred. The policy reason for this is that is that it cannot be determined with certainty if the doubtful loan will eventually go bad. However, as noted above, the risk premia, which are earned on loans, are taxed as they accrue. Accordingly, allowing a deduction for doubtful debts achieves a matching between the income and deductions.

The area of bad and doubtful debts is an important area of common concern to both regulators and tax administrators. For tax purposes, a link to regulatory reserves provides some protection against excessive claims. Amounts transferred to reserves reduce capital reported to the regulator and reduce income reported to shareholders, and so institutions would be reluctant to over-estimate such debts merely to reduce tax. And allowing such debts to give rise to tax deductions can provide an incentive to make such claims, so helping the regulator. (But, if a deferred tax debit is allowed with respect to a doubtful debt taken for regulatory purposes, this latter effect may be minimised.) However, regulatory reserves are generally conservative so simply using regulatory reserves for tax purposes may allow some deferral of tax. Some doubtful debts will eventually become fully paid off. It is for that reason that Canada allows a deduction for only 90 per cent of doubtful debts claimed for regulatory purposes. Bad debts are fully deductible.

1. Doubtful Debts (Specific provisions)

A doubtful debt or specific provision is taken when the financial institution determines that the value of the loan is impaired due to doubtful repayment. This may occur before the loan is determined to be bad and removed from company's books.

A specific provision is computed on a loan-by-loan basis based on the probability of recovery net of salvage value (partial write-off). In general it requires a precise estimation of the likely value of recovery. It therefore can be contrasted to a general provision, which is a form of contingency reserve taken to account for risks which may occur in the future. Some classes of small loans may have experience-rated reserves based on historical data. In this case the task of loan by loan determination would be burdensome, but there are enough similar loans that it is possible to estimate the number which are doubtful, based on the historical experience with that category of loan.

A variety of tests can be applied to determine whether a loan should be categorised as doubtful. These include:

- calculation and charging of interest has ceased and the account is closed (in suspense account);
- reminder notices have been issued and telephone and mail contact has been attempted without any success:
- a reasonable period has elapsed since the original due date for payment of debt (depends on type of credit whether 90, 120, 150 days overdue); and,
- formal demand notice has been served and no payment has been made.

2. When Is A Debt Bad?

The considerations to determine that a debt is bad are generally more stringent than for a doubtful debt. A debt is not bad until the debtor has:

- died without assets (or insufficient assets);

- cannot be traced and creditor is unable to ascertain the existence or whereabouts of any assets;

- become insolvent and estate has been distributed;

- the debt is statute barred and the debtor is relying on this as a defence (or may use as a defence);

- for corporate debtors, the creditor received final amounts from the liquidator or the debtor is wound up; and,

- judgement entered into on delinquent debtor

Rules are required for the recovery of previously claimed bad debts, if some value is eventually received.

3. Partial Write-offs

Financial accounting allows creditors to write down security if there is a permanent decline in the creditworthiness of a debtor. In the case of a doubtful debt, a partial write down would occur to the extent that there is a likelihood that there will be some recovery of value. Partial write-offs may occur in the establishment of a bad debt after the debtor sells its assets and transfers the proceeds to the creditor or the creditor seizes and liquidates debtor's assets. A partial write off may also occur after a debt for equity swap. In this case, the institution would write-off the difference between the loan's face value and the market value of the share. Where the debt is a security, the creditor might have to dispose of the security to realise a loss for tax purposes. On the other hand, in some countries, *i.e.* Germany and Austria, the creditor may write down the security to its market value in case of loss. Such treatment can be considered to be a form of hidden reserve since no corresponding adjustment is made in the case of an appreciation in the value of the security.

4. General Provisions

Regulators may require financial institutions to set aside general provisions, which are additional provisions for unidentified loan losses in the overall loan account. Examples would include; country risk provisions linked to countries with high sovereign debt or sector specific provisions based on the performance of a sector (*e.g.*, real estate). In such cases, the actual status of individual loans would not be taken into consideration. The EU Directive on Insurance permits the creation and maintenance of general provisions to a maximum general provision of 4 per cent of loans.

General provisions may be designed to smooth income as they provide pools of contingent deductions which can be used to cover exceptional losses on loans or securities. In such cases amounts that can be transferred into the reserve would be capped to a given percentage of income and specific provisions would be funded first out of the general reserve, before reducing income.

For the tax system the important question is whether general provisions should be deductible for tax purposes. In general they should not be as they represent a reserve for contingencies, rather than an actual decline in value. In some cases, general forms of provisioning have been allowed for tax purposes. For example during the sovereign debt crisis of the 1980's, a number of countries established regulatory categories of Sovereign debt which allowed a general reserve to be taken out against such loans. In this case, there had been an actual decline in value, but it was felt better to establish a general reserve rather than use specific provisions. The use of a general provision was felt necessary because of the thinly traded markets for such debts in which prices were variable and possibly undervalued and in order to avoid the need to write down specific loans, thereby possibly inviting partial repayment.

Reserves

Under ordinary tax accounting in many countries, expenses may not be recognised until they become fixed and determinable. Future expenses cannot therefore be recognised while there is still an element of contingency in their determination. The purpose of this rule is to avoid subjectivity and estimation, which provides opportunities for tax avoidance or deferral, can lead to disputes between taxpayers and tax administrators over the appropriate value to use and may result in an uneven application of tax among companies. On the other hand, insurance contracts, particularly for life insurance, give rise to liabilities which may not be realised for many years. Even for P&C insurance, where contracts generally are for one year, claims may not be settled or even reported for many years. On the other hand, the premium income associated with those future expenses is received and reported as income in the current year. A portion of the premium income is simply to fund future expected payments. It is similar to the receipt of the principal of a loan. Accordingly it is appropriate to set aside an amount in the form of a reserve to reflect the future repayment of that principal.

1. Accounting for Reserves

Reserves for future costs must be re-evaluated each year. Opening reserves are added to income and closing reserves are subtracted. In the example below, it is estimated in year one that 50 will be payable in year 3, and a reserve for that amount is set aside. As the opening reserve is zero this gives rise to a net deduction of 50 in the first year. In year two, the estimate of the expense has risen to 90. Accordingly a reserve of 90 is established, from which is deducted the opening reserve of 50 to yield a net deduction of a further 40. In year 3, an expense of 75 is actually incurred. Accordingly there is a deduction for the expense of 75 and an addition to income of the opening reserve of 90, yielding a net inclusion in income of 15.

Table 3. **Accounting for reserves**

		1	2	3
1	Estimated expense	50	90	..
2	Opening reserve	0	50	90
3	Closing reserve	50	90	0
4	Actual expense	0	0	75
	Net Income (2 – 3 – 4)	(50)	(40)	15

2. Discounting

In principle, future payments should not be reflected at face value. The cost to be deducted should reflect the time value of money. Accordingly, the reserve should be the discounted present value of the payment. Thus in the example above, the amounts to be deducted (calculated at a 10 per cent discount rate) would be:

Table 4. **Discounting**

		1	2	3
1	Estimated expense	50	90	–
2	Opening reserve	0	41.3	81.8
3	Closing reserve	41.3	81.8	0
4	Actual expense	0	0	75
	Net Income (2 – 3 – 4)	(41.3)	(40.5)	6.3

Using the face value of expenses overstates the value of the future expense today.

When using discounting, changes in reserves come from two sources. First the assumptions used to estimate the future expenses may change with the receipt of more information. For example, the total amount expected to be spent may be revised or the rate of interest at which the discount is to be calculated may change. Second, even with unchanged assumptions, the reserve will increase as the present value of the future expense rises with the passage of time. In the case where there is no change in the underlying costs, the increase in the reserve is simply the interest rate times the opening value of the reserve.

The opening value of the reserve at time, t, for an expense, E_T, payable at a future time, T, is:

$$R_t = E_T/(1 + i)^{(T - t)}$$

and at time t + 1 is:

$$R_{t + 1} = E_T/(1 + i)^{(T - (t + 1))}$$

so that:

Change in reserve = $R_{t + 1} - R_t = (1 + i)E_T/(1 + i)(1 + i)^{(T - (t + 1))} - E_T/(1 + i)^{(T - t)} = (1 + i) \cdot R_t - R_t = i \cdot R_t$

This amount represents a form of accrued interest expense for the insurance company which is comparable to the accrued interest on a discount bond. It is known as the inside or interest build up of the insurance policy and is an expense which funds the future policy claim.

It is interesting to note that in a case where amounts of assets and liabilities are being adjusted for inflation, in order to measure real income, that a similar adjustment should be made to the reserves as would be made to an ordinary debt liability. Failure to do so would ignore the benefit accruing to the company of the reduction in the real value of its future liabilities and so would overstate its costs and understate its income.

3. Transition

The issue of transition can arise when there are legislated changes in the methods of calculating reserves. At any given point in time, the current level of reserves will have built up over a considerable period of time. The net increase in the reserves is a fraction of the total reserves which have been established. If the expected future claims are smoothly increasing at rate, g, then the increase in reserves will be simply g $\cdot$ R_t. On the other hand, if reserves are to be recalculated due to a change in legislation, the entire amount of the change will occur in the first year in the absence of some form of transition, since reserves from the previous year (calculated under the old rules) are added back to income and this year's reserves (calculated under the new rules) are deducted. This amount could be large and it may be considered appropriate to provide some type of transitional relief. Four transition regimes are possible:

- **no transition**, where the new methods are applied to all policies beginning with the end of year calculation in the year the new mechanism comes into effect;
- **grandfathering**, where the new methods of reserving are only applied to newly issued policies;
- **a fresh start**, (where the policy induced change in base level of reserves is in effect ignored), by recalculating the beginning of the year reserves using the new methods without an income inclusion; and
- **a prorating** of the reserve inclusion arising from the recalculation over a number of years.

The argument for **no transition** would recognise that the amounts accumulated in reserves have already been deducted from income and represent a substantial and continuing deferral of tax. If it is determined that the reserves have been excessive, then immediate inclusion in income would end this deferral immediately. Immediate inclusion could give rise to a substantial payment of tax, (likely to exceed the current year's income, when the change in reserve is large).

Under **grandfathering**, the new reserving mechanism is not applied to any previously issued policies. This can be argued to be fair in that previously entered contracts can continue to enjoy the rules under which they were sold. However there are many changes in taxation of a general nature which apply to the results of decisions which were made in the past, (*i.e.* changes in tax rates). Moreover, the long duration of insurance policies implies that the deferral advantages inherent in the old rules would continue to benefit the industry for a long time, and would mean that little if any immediate tax revenues would result from the change. (The deferral does not end until the time when the amounts being reserved against are finally paid.) Finally, since the calculation of reserves affects company taxation, and not the direct interests of policyholders, in many cases it can be argued that the original contract between the company and the insured has not been adversely affected.

Under a **fresh start**, the opening balance of reserves would be calculated under the new rules, and the calculation of income for the year would use this new amount as the inclusion from prior year reserves. This has the effect of completely eliminating from income the change in reserving levels due to the new method. Obviously this is the policy which would be preferred by the industry. On the other hand, this change in the level of reserves reflects amounts that have already been deducted from income. Thus a fresh start would allow the industry to turn the deferral advantage of the over-reserving into a permanent reduction in tax. (In the absence of the change in reserve methods, the deferral on a given policy lasts until such time that the amounts being reserved against actually are paid. However for a growing company there is an effective permanent deferral of tax since the deferral losses on new business more than offset the recapture of the deferral losses on the old business.)

The intermediate position is to calculate current income with a recalculated opening reserve as under the fresh start approach. However rather than forgiving the total amount of the difference in reserving methods, this difference can be **prorated** and added to income over a reasonable period, (which depends on the size of the change and its impact relative to the income of the industry and the length of the deferral that would have resulted in the absence of the change). This method can be combined with the no transition method, if the prorationing is applied to the net of the change in reserving levels above loss-carry-forwards. No transition may be appropriate where deficiencies in the tax law, including overly generous reserves, have allowed a build up of losses (or unclaimed reserves) which are being carried forward from earlier years. In this case, amounts, which in part reflect the previous level of reserves, will be available to be deducted from present income. In such cases an immediate reserve inclusion could be required to the extent of these carry-forwards, bringing firms to taxation more quickly. No transition may also be appropriate when the insurance company has the ability to accelerate the payments made, leading to an unwinding of the reserve before the prorated amount has been included in income.

Chapter 4
ISSUES IN INTERNATIONAL TAXATION

International taxation issues have given rise to some of the most complex aspects of insurance company taxation. In some ways this is surprising since the traditional regulatory model of the insurance industry stresses the link between a company selling insurance and its customers. In many cases only resident companies could make sales of policies within a country. The intention of this type of restriction is to satisfy the prudential goal of ensuring that there are sufficient assets within the country to fund any claims which might arise under the policies written on behalf of resident policyholders. This link is further strengthened with mutual companies, where the policyholder is also in a sense the shareholder. And even stock companies have close equity-type links to their policyholders through the use of participating policies. Nevertheless, the existence of groups of companies that carry on an insurance business in different jurisdictions, often in the form of branches, and the variety of transactions that can be used to transfer value and income among jurisdictions has meant that international tax issues have been important and difficult.

Recent events are changing the international environment for insurance and, from the point of view of tax administrators, making a complex world even more complicated. As reported in a recent OECD publication, Liberalisation of International Insurance Operations,[1] the insurance industry has not escaped the liberalising trend in international trade in services. The major liberalising initiative have been the EU Third Insurance Directive, which has in principle allowed all classes of insurance to be placed on a cross-border basis among EU/EEA countries. In many countries in the OECD insurance contracts can now be written by non-residents if the insured initiates the contract, at least for certain types of business. While restrictions on trade do remain in the area of insurance services, further liberalisation can be expected.

This section provides a brief introduction to the issues in international taxation in the insurance industry, many of which are discussed in greater detail in the industry-specific sections that follow.

Allocating Income and Expenses

While the insurance industry has not traditionally been able to sell products across international borders, there has been a large amount of international investment by companies, either operating through offshore branches or subsidiaries in the foreign jurisdiction. Such international operations are natural, as there are risk diversification advantages for both the companies, who are not exposed to one market only, and to policyholders, who have the security of holding a policy offered by a large diversified company. As illustrated in the Table 5, for some countries in the OECD, the level of penetration of non-resident insurers is relatively large. And of course each non-resident insurer in one country represents an offshore branch or foreign subsidiary of a company resident in another. So a large share of most markets will be controlled by companies which have a connection with international operations. Finally, OECD countries are large net exporters of insurance services to non-OECD countries.

The problem this raises for tax administrators is to ensure that there is an appropriate matching between income and expenses with respect to policies in their jurisdiction. Net profit of an insurer is the difference between two relatively large numbers, income in the form of premiums and investment income, and expenses. Even small errors in their allocation across countries can lead to substantial understatement of profit in any given taxing jurisdiction.

---

1. Liberalisation of International Insurance Operations: Cross border Trade and the Establishment of Foreign Branches, OECD, 1999.

Table 5. **Foreign companies market share, non-life, 1997**[1]

	Foreign Market Share
Australia	32.9
Austria	49.2
Canada	63.7[2]
Czech Republic	28.4
Denmark	28.6
Finland	0.1
Germany	12.7
Hungary	90.9
Japan	3.6
Korea	0.4
Luxembourg	31.7
Mexico	11.0
Netherlands	24.0
Norway	21.0
Poland	15.0
Portugal	8.6
Spain	27.3
Turkey	8.7
United Kingdom	37.3
United States	8.8

1. Liberalisation of International Insurance Operations: Cross border Trade and the Establishment of Foreign Branches, OECD, 1999.
2. For the year 1996.

For certain types of income and expenses that are directly linked to specific policies, such as premiums, commissions and policy reserves, allocation is greatly simplified when the policy is sold by a resident insurer to a resident policyholder. Other costs, however, such as overheads or general borrowing cannot be linked to specific policies. Moreover, for some lines of business, *i.e.* multiyear life insurance and long-tail property insurance claims, there will be substantial investment income. Allocating this investment income across policies has proven to be very difficult. Simply relying on a regulatory approach such as the allocation of assets to jurisdictions leaves open various tax minimising strategies.

These already substantial problems will be exacerbated when policies can be more generally written across borders. In that case it will be necessary to allocate the costs and benefits within individual policies. In principle the functions of selling, administering and covering the risk of an insurance policies can be divided among a number categories, including:

- Advertising
- Commission on selling the policy
- Judging the risks of the policy
- Registering the policy
- Administering receipt of premiums
- Covering the risks of the policy
- Investing the net premiums
- Adjusting claims
- Paying claims
- Overheads, such as regulatory compliance, payroll, etc.

In particular, problems can arise when premiums are received in one jurisdiction, but indemnity losses occur in another jurisdiction or when underwriting losses are in one jurisdiction, but the associated investment income is in another. This can occur when business is written across national boundaries or through the use of reinsurance contracts. In such cases it important to ensure that there is an appropriate matching of income and expenses.

Attributing profits among jurisdictions would require allocating the appropriate portion of the profit to each of these components. In general, the OECD Model convention employs the principles as stipulated under Articles 7 and 9 of the convention. In that case the profits to be determined for a branch (or permanent establishment) of a non-resident company in a country are those which would arise if the branch were a separate entity. Under the independent entity principle found in Paragraph 2 of Article 7, the arm's length principle would be applied to the determination of the income attributable to the branch. This would be calculated on a transactional basis.

Such general principles may prove difficult to apply in all circumstances for the insurance industry. Accordingly, apportionment rules for certain circumstances are allowed under Paragraph 4 of Article 7. Currently, the OECD is examining the issue of whether Article 7(4) should be permitted as a way of attributing profit to a branch. A large number of OECD countries have concerns that it is not possible to apply such a formulary approach in a manner consistent with the arm's length principle.

Reinsurance

Reinsurance plays an important part in the management of risk by insurance companies. This is particularly the case for non-life companies, where reinsurance accepted represents over 10 per cent of total gross premiums.[2] Reinsurance contracts implicitly raise all of the cost allocation issues noted above and can be used to shift surplus and income. Between related parties, reinsurance raises the traditional issues of transfer pricing of ensuring that the premium received adequately covers the true costs of the insurance that is purchased. Between unrelated parties, reinsurance can be used for transferring losses between companies within a jurisdiction and for shifting income to be sheltered in offshore tax havens. Reinsurance is discussed in greater detail in its chapter.

Captive Insurance Companies

Insurance captives are insurance companies established in offshore jurisdictions, often by non-insurance companies (*e.g.* banks, large automobile makers or retailers). They started as way to self-insure risks that insurers would not assume (hazardous waste, toxic tort, or credit liability) or that the enterprise preferred to assume itself. In many jurisdictions non-insurance companies cannot establish tax reserves for such future contingent expenses. They may only recognise expenses when they become fixed and determinable. In such cases, a liability would be reported on the company's financial statements, but the company could not claim a reserve for tax purposes in respect of the future liabilities. (Insurance companies are allowed to establish reserves under special provisions.)

To avoid this situation, companies set up special purpose insurance subsidiaries (captives) to gain a deduction for premium payments to the insurer. The captives were established offshore to avoid domestic regulatory requirements and to avoid domestic tax on the profits arising from the transaction. This opens the opportunity to transfer assets and capital to the offshore captives to earn the investment income offshore and to shift income through transfer pricing arrangements that increase the deductible premiums paid.

Insurance firms may also establish offshore captive insurers to reinsure their policies, with the effect that underwriting profits and surplus, and its related investment income, are transferred to an offshore jurisdiction in a tax haven.

A number of tax provisions have been implemented to stop this type of tax avoidance.

The US IRS does not allow a deduction for premiums paid to another company (captive) within the same group as, by definition, no transfer of risk is possible within a corporate group. Companies that have offshore subsidiaries that offer insurance to non-related parties as well have challenged this treatment. In this case, the Court ruled that the premiums can be deducted if there is risk distribution,

---

2. *Insurance Statistics Yearbook, 1990-1997,* OECD, 1999: Table VII.3.

i.e. if the captive carries on an active insurance business with unrelated companies[3] – 30 per cent of gross premiums arising from unrelated businesses was sufficient.

A number of countries have introduced Controlled Foreign Corporation (CFC) legislation to tax this type of income on a current basis and prevent the deferral or non-taxation of this income.

The general treatment in the country of residence of the parent company of income earned in foreign subsidiaries is either to defer taxation of such income until it is repatriated in the form of a dividend or to exempt such income from domestic tax entirely. This treatment is consistent with the concept of capital import neutrality which requires that subsidiaries face the same tax rate as their competitors who are based in the foreign country, at least as long as the income is retained in that country. However, a number of OECD countries have systems designed to limit the tax-free accrual of "passive" income in offshore subsidiaries. The issues of competitiveness arising with active business income do not occur for passive income and such income, which would be taxed in the jurisdiction of residence, may be easily moved simply to avoid taxation. So anti-deferral regimes are explicit anti-avoidance devices, designed to protect the domestic tax base on mobile portfolio capital.

In a number of countries, profits earned by offshore insurance captives can be brought into this type of regime. For example, in the US, insurance income earned in a foreign subsidiary from insuring risks of related parties is included in the Sub-Chapter F accrual tax regime.

Should the regime apply only if the captive is in a tax haven? If so, how to define this? Possibilities include:

- countries with low statutory tax rates;

- countries with low effective tax rates;

- countries where the tax on the income would be "substantially" lower than in the country of residence; and,

- a list of "black" countries (or not in a list of "white" countries).

While the foreign subsidiary may be a captive, which has been established abroad in order to avoid taxation in the country of residence, it might be a legitimate insurance company operating independently of the parent company. In such cases the rule could inhibit the parent company from purchasing insurance from its subsidiary, even if it otherwise offered the most cost effective insurance policy. Accordingly, in some cases, the accrual tax regime is applied only if there is insufficient activity with unrelated companies, (*i.e.* 50 per cent share of revenues in the US).

Application of Tax Treaties

Tax treaties provide an important role in facilitating the conduct of business across national borders by codifying the relationship between the tax systems of different countries. Tax treaties cover a variety of issues including:

- the types of taxes to be considered to be income taxes and therefore eligible for double taxation relief;

- the determination of the country of residence of a taxpayer;

- methods of allocating profits among different jurisdictions; and,

- the treatment of different payments to non-residents.

A number of issues specific to insurance companies arise in the application of these provisions.

---

3. *AMERCO Subsidiaries v. Commissioner*, 96 T.C. 18 (1991), aff'd Slip.OP. No. 91-70732 (9th Cir. 11/5/92); *The Harper Group v. Commissioner*, 96 T.C. 45 (1991), aff'd Slip.OP. No. 91-70576 (9th Cir. 11/5/92); *Sears, Roebuck and Co v. Commissioner*, 96 T.C. 61 (1991), aff'd in part and rev'd in part Slip. OP. No. 91-3038 (7th Cir. 8/18/92);

1. *Double Taxation Relief*

One of the principle purposes of tax conventions is to prevent double taxation of the same income by two different jurisdictions. This can be done by assigning the right to tax exclusively to one jurisdiction, exempting foreign-sourced income in the country of residence of the taxpayer or by taxing such income, but allowing a credit against residence country taxes for taxes paid in the source country. One of the special features of insurance taxation is the variety of ways in which countries tax insurance, particularly life insurance. With such different taxes, some may not qualify as income taxes and so may not be creditable. For example Australia, Ireland and the U.K. use a form of I-E taxation, (described in the chapter on policyholder taxation), which taxes the investment profits accruing to both the company and the policyholder and Canada uses a minimum tax based upon the capital the company.

Problems can also arise in the taxation of income accruing to the policyholder. If the income arising in the insurance policy is taxable in the country of residence of the policyholder, but the policy is written by a company in another jurisdiction, double taxation may result. In some cases, taxes are paid by the company on behalf of the policyholder (Canada with the investment income tax (IIT), Denmark with its real interest rate tax and with the I-E tax). Such taxes would not be creditable against any policyholder taxation arising in the policyholder's home jurisdiction. These types of issues will become more prevalent as more policies are written across national borders. (In fact the United Kingdom no longer applies its I-E tax on such policies to address this issue.)

2. *Permanent Establishment*

In order to determine if a company has enough presence in a country so that it should be taxable in that country for taxation purposes, the OECD Model Tax Convention has adopted the concept of a permanent establishment (Article 5). In general a permanent establishment means a fixed place of business. Under the traditional regulatory regime, where a clear link must be established between the insurer and the jurisdiction where policies are to be sold, most insurance operations would be carried out through a permanent establishment. However for some types of business, or in the case where regulations now allow insurance policies to be sold across borders, other paragraphs of the Article would need to be relied upon if a state where to be able to tax the income of a company selling policies in its jurisdiction. For industries, such as the insurance industry, which often make sales through agents, paragraph 5 of the Article has introduced the concept of an agency relationship which is sufficient to be considered to be a permanent establishment. It states, "where a person – other than an agent of an independent status to whom paragraph 6 applies – is acting on behalf of an enterprise and has, and habitually exercises, in a Contracting State an authority to conclude contracts in the name of the enterprise, that enterprise shall be deemed to have a permanent establishment in that State in respect of any activities which that person undertakes for the enterprise". For these purposes an independent agent is, "a broker, general commission agent or any other agent of an independent status, provided that such persons are acting in the ordinary course of their business".

When applied to the typical manner of conducting business in the insurance industry the strict application of these concepts can lead to problems. Paragraph 6 of the Commentary on Article 5 of the OECD Model Treaty states.

"According to the definition of the term 'permanent establishment' an insurance company of one State may be taxed in the other State on its insurance business, if it has a fixed place of business within the meaning of paragraph 1 or if it carries on business through a person within the meaning of paragraph 5. Since agencies of foreign insurance companies sometimes do not meet either of the above requirements, it is conceivable that these companies do large-scale business in a State without being taxed in that State on their profits arising from such business. In order to obviate this possibility, various conventions concluded by OECD Member countries include a provision which stipulates that insurance companies of a State are deemed to have a permanent establishment in the other State if they collect premiums in that other State through an agent established there-other than an agent who already constitutes a permanent establishment by virtue of paragraph 5-or insure risks situated in that territory through such an agent. The decision as to whether or not a provision along these lines should be included in a convention will depend on the factual and legal situation prevailing in the Contracting States concerned."

Chapter 5

TAXATION OF PROPERTY AND CASUALTY INSURANCE COMPANIES

This section will concentrate on the business and tax policy aspects of P&C or general insurance. The P&C business is a purer insurance business than the life insurance business as its contracts are generally of a short term (one year) and do not have an explicit savings motive. For this reason, the taxation of P&C insurance has generally been less problematic than the taxation of life insurance. Nevertheless many basic concepts are shared with the life insurance business, particularly for certain types of risks, and so form a useful introduction to the calculation of income for tax purposes for life insurance.

Types of P&C Insurance Policies

Property and casualty insurance policies generally relate to the risk of financial loss due to accident (third party or damage to property), theft, and natural disasters such as fires, storms, wind, and earthquakes. Lines of business usually required to be identified by insurance regulators are as follows:

- motor,
- property (industrial, commercial, residential),
- marine, aviation and transport,
- professional indemnity (medical, legal, engineering),
- workers compensation,
- credit and surety.

Computation of Insurance Premium

Insurance premiums will be set at a level which covers the insurer's expected costs of claims, its costs of administration (including sales commissions) and a profit return. The amount of profit required will vary according to the perceived degree of under-writing risk for the different lines of business. The degree of risk may also depend upon the locality of the risk (*i.e.* a high crime area), the nature of the insured (*i.e.* higher premiums for young drivers) or the possibility of exceptionally large claims (natural disasters).

Premiums may be written many years before the settlement of claims for some lines of business. The insurer may dispute settlement of the claim; settlement may be on a periodic basis; or claims may be incurred but not reported (IBNR) for some disease related cover (see below).

The "prepayment" of premiums in respect of future claims is similar to a loan from the insured to the insurer. The insurer invests the premiums to earn investment income to help fund future claims. Accordingly, the premium is lower than the ultimate cost of future expected claims, expenses and profit margin, as these amounts must be discounted back to the time that the premium is paid to reflect the time value of money.

While discounting is part of the pricing of a policy, *i.e.* setting the premium, its use for accounting is less widespread and even more limited in the case of taxation. Lack of discounting provides a hidden reserve to insurers, as discussed below.

Accounting of Income

P&C insurers report two elements of income: underwriting and investment returns. Underwriting income is the insurer's net income excluding returns and gains on investments. It is accrued with the use of reserves (technical provisions). This split is historical, and may be one source of the conservative accounting noted above, since in reality the earning of investment income (on premiums, if not capital) is an intrinsic part of the insurance business. Underwriting income may vary because premiums are low due to cyclical competition, the policies are new business with little historic claims experience, there is a high volatility of claims (large standard deviation) or due to catastrophic claims (natural, environment or nuclear).

In many countries accounting guidelines are provided by the insurance regulators, rather than using Generally Accepted Accounting Principals (GAAP). In the Economic Union, the Insurance Accounts Directive 91/674/EEC (IAD) provides guidelines for financial reporting. These rules are supplemented by individual country practice that can differ widely, even within the EU.

Insurers are allowed a number of different types of reserves. The nature of the insurance business is the acceptance and intermediation of risks. These risks are funded by premiums that are included in the income of the insurer. It is accordingly appropriate under the matching and accrual principles that the insurer can reflect a provision, or reserve, for the future claims and expenses. Other reserves are allowed for technical reasons to provide a better matching of income and expenditure. This treatment contrasts with the treatment in many countries of other types of business, where reserves are not allowed and expenses can only be recognised when they become fixed, determinable and legally binding.

Simplified Example

The basic mechanics of insurance reserves, and the taxation issues that arise from them, can be illustrated with a series of simple examples. In the following tables the following assumptions are made:

- The duration of the insurance contract is for one year.
- The premium of 100 is payable at the inception of the contract, assumed to be July 1.
- Expenses of 20 are incurred in establishing the contract.
- All claims of 90 are paid out 2½ years after inception of the contract.
- Funds invested earn a 10% return.

Cashflow

The following table outlines the cashflows that are receivable in the above example. If all receipts and expenses were accounted for only as they become due and payable, the insurer would report a substantial profit in the first year, and a large loss in the final year, illustrating the need for a more sophisticated accrual accounting in order to match income and expenses.

Table 6. **Cashflow**[1]

		1	2	3
1	Premiums written (due and receivable)	100	0	0
2	Expenses (due and payable)	20	0	0
3	Claims (due and payable)	0	0	90
4	Underwriting cash flow (1 – 2 – 3)	80	0	–90
5	Investment return	4	8.4	9.2
	Cash flow (4 + 5)	84	8.4	–80.8

1. Line 5: Year 1 has only six months between inception and the accounting year end resulting in interest of 4 = (.5 x 10 % x 80). At the end of the first year, assets are the net premium of 80 plus the investment return of 4.

Income and Balance Sheet Statements

In order to more properly reflect the annual income of the insurer, accrual accounting techniques must be employed. The basic adjustments which must be made to cashflows in order to arrive at a figure for profits are:

- *Unearned premium reserves* – to spread the premium over the term of the contract, to match it to the presumed accrual of risks;
- *Outstanding losses reserves* – to reflect claims as they are incurred, rather than paid; and,
- *Deferral of acquisition expenses* – to match the acquisition costs to the period that the premium income is recognised.

1)   Unearned Premium Reserves

The unearned premium reserve defers a portion of the premium that is due and receivable from the policyholder in the current accounting year to the next accounting year in order to match the premium income to the time that the risks are outstanding. The concept of due and receivable usually starts from the time the underwriter (or the broker acting on the insurer's behalf) agrees to underwrite a person. (In some countries the premiums are reported when received.) Whether premiums are payable at the inception of the contract or on a periodic basis *(e.g.,* semi-annually or monthly), all of the premium is due and receivable in the year of the contract's inception (at the point of the insurer's acceptance which may be before the first premium is paid). This reserve computation assumes that claims are *incurred uniformly* over the contract period *or cannot be predicted using historic data*. There are three apportionment methods: percentage apportionment, 24th basis, and daily basis.

Percentage apportionment defers a fixed proportion (say 50%) of premiums to the subsequent accounting year. The *24*th *basis* defers premiums based on an allocation of premiums on a fortnightly basis (if the year end is December 31, the unearned premium reserve for policies written on February 14 would be 3/24th of premium written on February 14). *Daily basis* defers premiums according to the day they were written (44/365 for premiums written on February 14), and is the most appropriate method under the assumption of an even spread risks (and easily calculable in the age of computers).

Some types of P&C insurance business do not exhibit uniform distribution of (incurred) claims over the contract period and therefore the simple unearned premium reserve is not appropriate. In this instance an insurer may be permitted to set aside an additional reserve – a reserve for unexpired risks – where historic data supports the assumption that claims increase over the contract period. This is determined by computing the ratio of claims incurred to earned premiums for a number of years. These reserves are usually accepted for tax purposes.

2)   Outstanding Claims

An outstanding claims reserve is established for events that *have* occurred. Outstanding claims is the total amount of claims incurred, but not yet paid, at the end of the accounting year. There are two parts to outstanding losses:

- *Claims reserves* are losses reported and computed on a case by case basis, with the amount likely to be paid out on each claim being separately estimated. (Also called *losses reserves*)
- *Incurred But Not Reported Reserve (IBNR)* are claims that were incurred but not reported as at the end of the accounting year. These claims require an actuarial estimate based on historic data.

Outstanding claims should include direct policy costs[1] and should be net (*i.e.,* reduced) by the value of the property after salvage or subrogation.[2]

IAD permits discounting for financial reporting purposes where the average settlement is date is 4 years or more (using prudential assumptions). Discounting for tax is required in some countries.

---

1. Direct policy costs include claim investigation and assessment costs and direct claim settlement costs.
2. Subrogation is the right of an insurer to seek compensation from the person who caused the insured damage.

Not all claims have been reported at the time an insurer draws up their books of account. Such losses are reflected in the IBNR. In some cases this may reflect delays in the reporting of claims. In other cases, it may reflect the fact that an insurable event has occurred, without the insured being aware of it. Therefore the claim may occur after several years, at the time that the problem becomes apparent. Major sources of IBNRs are diseases that take a long time to develop. A claim is incurred when a disease is contracted (*i.e.* when exposed to a nuclear disaster or asbestos) and not later when the disease manifests itself, which is the event that establishes the right to a claim. It is the insurer at the time of the exposure that is liable to settle the claim, not the insurer at the time that the disease is diagnosed. Consequently, an insurer must establish an IBNR reserve for claims that may be reported in the future once the disease is detected and a claim reported.

3) Prepaid Expenses

Prepaid expenses are acquisition costs and other costs of underwriting new business including commissions paid to agents and brokers, premium taxes, marketing and research expenses.

The treatment of prepaid expenses under accrual accounting is to defer the recognition of the expenses until the period to which the services that are received for them occur. In the case of insurance, this occurs over the period of coverage. The ratio to be used parallels that used for the income received in the form of premiums.

(An alternative way of recognising prepaid expenses is to reduce the unearned premium reserve as a way of matching acquisition costs with earned premiums, *i.e.*:

Net unearned premium reserve = (100 – 20)/2 = 40

Earned premium (year 1) = 100 – 40 = 60

The accrual accounting for a claims, expenses and unearned premiums is illustrated in the following example.

Most countries require that prepaid expenses be spread over the contract period for tax purposes. Some countries require that prepaid expenses be deferred for a fixed period, (three years in Italy). On the other hand, Germany and Austria do not require deferral of expenses over the contract period. This provides a tax incentive for the insurance industry. The next table shows what would happen if the expenses were not deferred. A loss would be created in the first year, to be offset by higher profits in the second. While over the period total taxable income would be the same, a deferral of tax results.

Table 7. **Accrual accounting**[1]

		1	2	3
	Income statement			
1	Earned premiums	50	50	
2	Expenses	10	10	
3	Claims incurred	45	45	0
4	Underwriting profit (1 – 2 – 3)	–5	–5	0
5	Investment return	4	8.4	9.2
	Profit (4 + 5)	–1	3.4	9.2
	Balance sheet			
7	Investments	84	92.4	11.6
8	Prepaid expenses	10		
9	Unearned premium reserve	50	0	
10	Outstanding claims	45	90	0
	Profit/Loss balance	–1	2.4	11.6

1. Line 1: Earned premiums is equal to direct written premiums (100) less the change in unearned premium reserve.
   Line 3: The claims incurred ratio (claims incurred/earned premiums) is constant at 90 %.
   Line 7: The value of investments is total underwriting cash flows (premiums minus expenses) plus accrued interest income.
   Line 8: Half of acquisition expenses are deferred to year 2 to match premiums and reported separately.
   Line 9: Unearned premium reserve is 50 % of gross direct written premiums.
   Line 11: The profit and loss balance shows the total accumulated profits – current year and those brought forward from prior years – that have not been distributed to shareholders or policyholders.

Table 8. **Undeferred prepaid expenses**

		1	2	3
1	Earned premiums	50	50	
2	Expenses	20	0	
3	Claims incurred	_45_	_45_	_0_
4	Underwriting profit (1 – 2 – 3)	–15	5	0
5	Investment return	_4_	_8_	_9_
	Profit (**4 + 5**)	–11	13.4	9.2

4) Reserve for Unexpired Risks

The reserve for unexpired risks is used when claims are not incurred uniformly and the claims pattern can be determined actuarially. Where the insurer defers acquisition expenses, more prepaid expenses are deferred to subsequent years of income. This will ensure that the claims incurred ratio (claims incurred ÷ earned premiums) and the expense ratio (expenses ÷ earned premiums) are constant over the term of the contract. In some cases reserves for unexpired risks are used to recognise that premiums are insufficient to cover future liabilities. To the extent that this effectively results in an anticipation of future claims, a deferral of tax would result.

Table 9. **Reserve for unexpired risks**[1]

		1	2	3
	Income statement			
1	Earned premiums	33.3	66.7	
2	Expenses	6.7	13.3	
3	Claims incurred	_30_	_60_	_0_
4	Underwriting profit (1 – 2 – 3)	–3.3	–6.7	0
5	Investment return	_4.0_	_8.4_	_9.2_
6	Profit (**4 + 5**)	0.7	1.7	9.2
	Claims incurred to earned premiums	90%	90%	
	Balance sheet			
7	Investments	84	92.4	11.6
8	Prepaid expenses	13.3		
9	Reserve for unexpired risks	66.7	0	
10	Outstanding claims	30	90	0
	Profit/Loss balance	0.7	2.4	11.6

1. Line 8: A portion of expenses are deferred to year 2 (66.7/100 x 20 = 13.3)
   Line 9: Reserve for unexpired risk is often reported as: unearned premium reserve (50) plus additional reserve for unexpired risks (17) reserve. The claims incurred ratio should be constant.

5) Discounting

One of the more controversial issues in accounting for P&C insurance for both tax and regulatory purposes is discounting, that is reducing future claims by an interest factor when computing reserves for future payments. From an economic point of view discounting is appropriate. This is consistent with the important role that the time value of money plays in determining premiums and is the counterpoint to the large amounts of investment income earned by insurers. For regulatory purposes the lack of discounting perhaps reflects the natural conservatism of actuaries and regulators, both of whom would like to avoid nasty surprises. For tax purposes, the industry would obviously prefer the method that delays the payment of tax, *i.e.* non-discounting. However, when future claims are not discounted, then there is a deferral of tax and an implicit tax incentive for the industry.

43

Table 10. **Discounting**

		1	2	3
	Income statement			
1	Earned premiums	50	50	
2	Expenses	10	10	
3	Claims incurred (discounted)	<u>37.2</u>	<u>44.6</u>	<u>8.2</u>
4	Underwriting profit $(1 - 2 - 3)$	2.8	−4.6	−8.2
5	Investment return	<u>4</u>	<u>8.4</u>	<u>9.2</u>
6	Profit $(4 + 5)$	6.8	3.8	1.1
	Claims incurred ratio 3/1	74 %	89 %	
	Claims incurred			
12	Outstanding claims reserve (closing balance)	37.2	81.8	0
13	Outstanding claims reserve (opening balance)	0	37.2	81.8
14	Claims (due and payable)	<u>0</u>	<u>0</u>	<u>90</u>
15	Claims incurred $(12 - 13 + 14)$	37.2	44.6	8.2
	Discount factor/$(1.10)^{T-1}$	0.826	0.909	

Insurers in Australia, Canada, and USA are required to discount future claims. Germany, Portugal, Greece, the UK and Luxembourg do not discount. Other EC members discount long-tail business (4 or more years average settlement date, Article 60 of IAD).

6) *Discounting with margins*

Another area on potential controversy between regulators and actuaries on one hand and tax authorities on the other is the treatment of margins for adverse deviations. The actuarial profession would include a margin for adverse deviation (prudence margin) in computing discounted reserves – thus increasing the reserve and lowering profit. From the conservative point of view of regulators, this is prudent and increases the margin of error in ensuring solvency. The margin is in fact a form of hidden capital or contingency reserve. However from a tax point of view, a deferral of tax again results, on average, and so such margins are not appropriate for taxation purposes. Nevertheless, unwinding such calculations may prove to be difficult and so other *ad hoc* adjustments could be made, as in Canada, where tax reserves are equal to 95% of the lesser of the regulatory reserves and actuarial liabilities.

In the example, a margin is added to future expected claims (+10%) in case claims experience is worse than expected in the premium calculation and deducted from the discount interest rate (–1%), in case investment experience is worse than expected. Most of the profit is not recognised until the completion of the entire contract, *i.e.* when the insurer is "released from risk".

Table 11. **Discounting with margins**

		1	2	3
1	Earned premiums	50	50	
2	Expenses	10	10	
3	Claims incurred $(1.1 \times 90/1.09^{T-1})$	<u>41.7</u>	<u>49.2</u>	<u>−0.8</u>
4	Underwriting profit $(1 - 2 - 3)$	−1.7	−9.2	0.8
5	Investment return	<u>4</u>	<u>8.4</u>	<u>9.2</u>
6	Profit $(4 + 5)$	2.3	−0.8	10.1
	Claims incurred ratio 3/1	83 %	98 %	
	Claims incurred			
7	Outstanding claims (current)	41.7	90.8	0
8	Outstanding claims (prior)	0	41.7	90.8
9	Claims (due and payable)	<u>0</u>	<u>0</u>	<u>90</u>
10	Claims incurred $(7 - 8 + 9)$	41.7	49.2	−0.8
	Discount factor $(1.10)/(1.09)$-year	0.842	0.917	

Table 12. **Comparison of profit methods**

		1	2	3
1	Deferred taxation model	−11.0	13.4	9.2
2	Capitalised costs, undiscounted	−1.0	3.4	9.2
3	Capitalised costs, discounted	6.8	3.8	1.1
4	Capitalised costs, discounted with margins	2.3	−0.8	10.1

Comparison of Profit Methods

The various methods of computing profit yield markedly different patterns of income recognition.

The deferred taxation model 1) does not defer prepaid expenses and does not discount outstanding claims and so creates a large upfront loss when the policy is initiated allowing income on other policies to be sheltered. This is a deferral of tax, but with a growing company the result is a permanent reduction in the effective taxes paid as new policies are continually entered into to shelter the recapture of the deferred income of the older policies. The use of technical reserves to match acquisition costs with premium income in the capitalised costs model 2) provides a smoother recognition of profit over the period at risk. However significant deferral of tax remains as outstanding claims are recognised at the ultimate cost rather than taking into account the time value of money. Discounting of outstanding claims 3) brings forward profit to the years the claims are incurred, and is the method which is the most favourable to the tax system as it eliminates deferrals. Discounting outstanding claims with margins for adverse deviation 4) reports profit as the insurer is released from risks. This method again has the effect of deferring profit recognition relative to the full accrual method embodied in the capitalised costs, discounted model. Each approach generates the same 11.6 of total profit over the period.

Other Reserves

Many jurisdictions allow P&C insurers to deduct a reserve for some future contingent risks (claims that have not been incurred as at the end of the accounting year). These reserves include:

- *equalisation reserves* for business with a high (historic) standard deviation of claims;
- *catastrophic reserve* for low probability/high financial loss insured events;
- *rate stabilisation reserves* for termination risks of group business;
- *investment valuation reserves* for the possible (contingent) decline in the value of assets.

1) Equalisation Reserves

Some countries require the deduction of an equalisation reserve for tax and accounting purposes to reduce underwriting volatility. In Germany, for example, the reserve is required for lines that have a standard deviation of claims incurred ratio of more than 5% over the prior 15 years (30 years for hail, credit, guarantee and fidelity insurance). The maximum reserve is 450% of the standard deviation of claims incurred ratio multiplied by earned premiums – the 450% factor represents the present value of expected above average claims experience. (A 600% factor applies for hail, credit guarantee and fidelity insurance.) While regulators would like this type of reserve as it smoothes income flows in a notably volatile industry, there is little tax justification for equalisations reserves, particularly when adequate loss carry-overs are provided.

2) Catastrophic Reserves

Some insurable events have a low probability of occurrence but a large financial loss if the event occurs (natural disasters and systemic credit risks). Many regulators require insurers to deduct a provision for catastrophic losses. The increase in the catastrophic reserve offsets the additional risk load in the premium, and therefore has a theoretical justification. If the provision is permitted, the maximum reserve and annual transfers in and out are usually an arbitrary proportion of premiums.

The argument against a catastrophic reserve is that it is not possible to compute a reasonable actuarial estimate of an insurer's liability. The amount of claims and the probability of a catastrophic event cannot be predicted. Moreover, most insurers attempt to limit the impact of catastrophes through reinsurance, and so the catastrophic reserve should, in principle, be reduced by any reinsurance of the risk. Even if no catastrophic reserve is allowed, the correct present value of tax is collected when the claims are only recognised as they are incurred. In such cases adequate loss carryovers would be needed to allow an insurer to fully offset the resulting loss.

3) Rate Stabilisation Reserves

Premiums for large group insurance policies are often computed solely on the experience of the group. That is, the premiums and claims of the group are not pooled with other group plans.

The insurer has little *underwriting risk* under these large group plans due to the law of large numbers. However, there is a *termination risk* that can result in a loss for the insurer because the policyholder can terminate the policy before the insurer has recovered its losses. The insurer may reduce the termination risk by conditionally crediting the policyholder a refund of premiums for favourable (low) claims experience until the end of the contract period; or until conditional refunds are large enough to exceed any reasonable termination loss.

The insurer will set aside amounts that it has conditionally credited to the policyholder in a rate stabilisation reserve (claims fluctuations reserve) and will credit interest to the policyholder and the reserve. Stabilisation reserves can be a source of tax deferral if the policyholder deducted the premiums in computing income unless the income credited to the fund is allocated to the insured for tax purposes. The reserves should be equal to the present value of the expected termination losses.

4) Investment Valuation Reserves

Financial reporting allows/requires insurers to report an investment valuation reserve. The reserve is an appropriation of surplus. It is intended to set aside some a portion of surplus for the possibility that investment returns may fall. There is little if any tax policy justification for such reserves.

Another approach used by Germany, Austria and a few other countries is to allow companies to report investments at the lower of their cost or current market value. Both cases under-report investment earnings. This will result in deferrals for tax purposes.

Outstanding Claims Computation

Auditors will look at a pattern of assumed claims settlement over time to judge whether the assumptions by a company are consistent over time. If they are not then the auditors will require a satisfactory explanation of the differences. The runoff of outstanding claims over a development period is computed using a triangulation method. For any category of business the ratios among the years will be expected to remain constant.

Table 13. **Outstanding claims computation**

Under-writing Year	Claims Reported	Development year		
		t + 1	t + 2	t + 3
t	54	16.3	10.9	5.4
t – 1	50	9.9	5.0	
t – 2	45	4.5		
Total		30.7	15.8	5.4

Note: Annual growth of reported claims is 10%.

Different categories of business exhibit different patterns of claim settlement. Short tail business is where claims are reported and settled within a short time (12 months) after occurrence of the insured event. Examples would include auto collision. Long tail business is where there is a lengthy delay between the underwriting year and either the emergence or settlement of claims, or both. Examples would include certain types of illness or third party liabilities that may involve lengthy court proceedings.

Chapter 6

COMPARISONS OF SELECTED OECD COUNTRIES: TREATMENT OF GENERAL INSURANCE UNDER THE INCOME TAX[1]

	Income tax rate[1]	Discounting	Equalisation reserve	Catastrophe reserve
Australia	36%, will be reduced to 30% by 2001	Yes, more than 4 year payout	No	No
Austria	34%	No	Based on specific rules, (historical standard deviation, annual premiums in the current and prior two years, 2 Mio., ATS, etc.)	
Belgium	40.2%	No	No	Natural hazard: 350% of premiums net of reinsurance Air and space: 350% of premiums net of reinsurance Assault and labour dispute: 350% of premiums net of reinsurance Environmental pollution: 500% of premiums net of reinsurance Product liability: 500% of premiums net of reinsurance
Canada	38 – 46%, (varies by province)	Yes	No	Nuclear: 100% of premiums net of reinsurance less commissions Earthquake: 75% of premiums net of reinsurance
Finland	28%	n.a.	Based on historic standard deviations	No
Germany	40% plus local taxes	No	Conditions: 1) annual premiums in current and prior 2 years exceed DM 250 000 2) business not reinsured 3) one underwriting loss in last 15 years 4) standard deviation of claims over prior 15 years exceeds 5% of average claims for that period. Annual additional reserve = (current year claim – the historical average experience)* current year earned premiums + 3.5% notional investment return Maximum cumulative reserve = current year earned premium * 450% * standard deviation (see 4 above)	Nuclear

1. Data in tables updated to October 1999.

	Income tax rate[1]	Discounting	Equalisation reserve	Catastrophe reserve
Ireland	28%	No	No	No
Italy	37%	No	Compulsory technical reserves deductible	Compulsory technical reserves deductible
Luxembourg	30%	No	Permitted (as required by regulator) for special types of insurance with large varying risk factors (*e.g.* credit, hail) as a percentage of net premiums	Only for reinsurance business Overall limit is a per cent of average net premiums over a 5 year period, varying from 1 250% to 2 000% according to line of business Transfers to reserve may not create a loss and transfers from reserve are required when line of business incurs loss
Mexico	35%	No	No	Earthquake and Volcano eruption Insurance: 100% of premiums Tax Deductible Allowance
Netherlands	35%	No	Maximum annual transfer to reserve is lesser of – 0.09% of mathematical reserve – 22.5% of retained profit – taxable profit in the year Reserve must be reduced if: – other reserves strengthened – debit balance of net capital gains or loss in the year. Total reserve can not exceed 22.5% of net premiums	Nuclear Annual additions to reserve are the lesser of 50% profits on nuclear related risks, and retained profits (before the reserve). Total reserve may not exceed total amount insured for these risks.
New Zealand	33%	No	No	No
Portugal	37.4%	No	Permitted as required by regulator	No
Spain	35% (25% for mutuals and 20% for co-operatives)	No	Permitted as required by regulator	No
Sweden	28%	No	Credit insurance as required by regulator For other classes of insurance a reserve, calculated as percentages of premiums written and of provisions for outstanding claims, is allowed, up to a maximal level.	
Switzerland	35%	No (unless approved by regulator)	No	For some lines of business – mandatory for credit and motor liability as required by regulator
United Kingdom	No	No		Annual transfers to reserve as a percentage of net written premiums are: Property (3%), pecuniary loss (3%),pecuniary loss mortgage (12%), marine and aviation (6%), nuclear (75%), non-proportional reinsurance (11%)

	Income tax rate[1]	Discounting	Equalisation reserve	Catastrophe reserve
United Kingdom (*cont.*)	30%			Maximum reserves as a percentage of net written premiums of prior 5 years are: Property (20%), pecuniary loss (20%),pecuniary loss mortgage (150%), marine and aviation (40%), nuclear (600%), non-proportional reinsurance (75%)
United States	35% plus state and local	Yes (discount and claims payout rates are prescribed)	Credit insurance. Same as regulatory reserve (50% of premiums) except that funds must be invested in federal non-interest bearing "tax and loss" bonds Reserves must be added back into revenue no later than 10 years	No

1. See additional tables for details.

Chapter 7

TAXATION AND REINSURANCE

Introduction

Reinsurance is a mechanism through which insurers can manage risks by shifting them to other insurers in exchange for the payment of a premium. By allowing insurers to tailor their risks, it plays an important role in the efficient functioning of insurance markets in OECD countries. Reinsurance can be particularly important in the process of establishing viable insurance markets in economies where an insurance industry has not previously existed as it is a means for start up firms to offload risks for which they have insufficient capital. However, as with many other financial products, it can be the source of manipulation and tax avoidance if it not properly treated within in the tax system. As always, the challenge is to find a system of taxation of reinsurance which does not inhibit its important contribution to the establishment of an insurance market while at the same time is not vulnerable to tax avoidance.

The Basic Mechanics of Reinsurance

The reinsurance market has a number of actors. The first is the **Insurer** or **Direct Writer** of the policy. The insurer writes the policy for the policyholder and is contractually responsible for any payments to the policyholder that come due under the policy, even if those risks are eventually covered as part of a reinsurance contract. The insurer markets the policy, bears the costs of its sale and on-going administration and receives the premium income associated with the policy.

In a reinsurance contract, the insurer (**Cedant**) cedes the risks to a **Reinsurer** in return for the payment of the reinsurance premium. As the contract is between the insurer and the reinsurer, any claims arising from the contract give rise to payments between those two parties. The insurer remains responsible for settling any claims with respect to the original insurance contract.

A reinsurer may in turn reinsure the risks that it takes on through a **Retrocession** of risks to a **Retrocessionaire**. Such arrangements allow a reinsurer in turn to manage the risks which it takes on.

Types of Risks Covered under Reinsurance

Depending upon the type of reinsurance contract which is written, a number of types of risk can be transferred from the direct writer to the reinsurer. While all of these risks could be present in a typical reinsurance contract, depending upon the terms and conditions of the contract some may not be. The types of risks that are transferred will be related to the underlying motivation of the reinsurance contract.

The most basic risk which can be reinsured is the **Underwriting Risk** that claims will be more than expected and so the premiums which have been received by the insurer will be insufficient to cover all of the claims which are made under the policy (or group of policies). This type of risk arises most typically in types of P&C business that can experience volatility in claims experience and for which it can be difficult to establish an appropriate premium. A particular example occurs where there is the possibility of major catastrophic events which may give rise to a very large single claim, a nuclear power plant disaster or a failed satellite launch, or an unexpectedly large number of related claims, such as after an earthquake or hurricane. Accordingly the major motivation for entering into reinsurance contracts which involve the transfer of significant amounts of underwriting risk is to protect the insurer

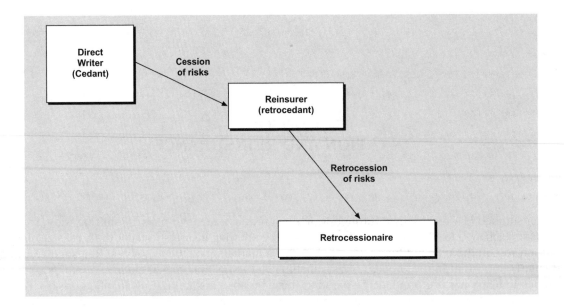

from events which could have the possibility of endangering its profitability and possibly solvency. They have the benefit of reducing the capital required to support the business written by the insurer.

Reinsurance contracts can also be used to manage other types of risk, which can arise after the basic claim has been submitted, but before it is finally settled. **Timing Risk** arises from the possibility that the payment of claims may occur before expected, therefore increasing the present value of the claims stream. Reinsurance can fix the present value of the claims at the amount of the premium that is paid. **Investment Risk** arises due to the possibility that the yield on investments may be lower than expected. In such cases the funds set aside in reserves to pay the future claims settlement will be insufficient. Again, the use of reinsurance matches the value of premiums to the present value of the claims.

Finally, for certain types of reinsurance contracts, the reinsurer shares in the cost of administering the policy. In this case, the **Expense Risk** that administrative expenses exceed amounts expected is transferred.

In addition, the reinsurer assumes a **Credit Risk** that the insurer may not pay premiums when due, that subrogation rights may not be enforceable or that the retrocessionaire may be unable to pay amounts owing on subsequent reinsurance taken out by the reinsurer. On the other hand, reinsurance contracts introduce a new credit risk for the insurer; that the reinsurer does not in fact make good on its obligations.

Types of Reinsurance Arrangements

There are two basic forms of the reinsurance agreements: reinsurance treaties and facultative reinsurance.

Under a **Reinsurance Treaty**, a one-year contract is undertaken where the reinsurer agrees in advance to accept a specified amount of all risks or losses defined in the treaty. Accordingly, the reinsurer does not have the right to examine and select from among those risks that meet the defined risks under the contract.

With a **Facultative Reinsurance Contract**, the reinsurer assesses each policy before agreeing to assume risks. Facultative reinsurance is usually limited to large insurance policies.

Under either type of contract, the reinsurer and insurer will share risks on some agreed basis. There are two main types of risk sharing arrangements. The first are **Proportional Reinsurance Arrangements** – where a constant proportion of each risk is shared – in effect an insurance partnership. In this case reinsurance acts to reduce the overall size of the risks retained by the insurer, for all patterns of claim. For example this can be used when the capital available to the insurer is limited relative to its capacity to market policies.

Non-Proportional Reinsurance Arrangements, on the other hand, can be used to limit the maximum risk faced by an insurer. This has the effect of protecting the insurer from those types of events, which would directly affect its solvency, while maintaining the risks associated with more normal claims patterns. These limitations can operate in a number of different ways. For example under "per risk excess of loss" reinsurance, the insurer retains risks up to a maximum amount per claim (such as 20 000). The reinsurer would pay any claim above that amount. Some agreements have limits on the amount payable by the reinsurer for any particular event (an occurrence limit) which may give rise to a number of claims triggered by the same event. Under a **Per Occurrence Limit**, the reinsurer accepts risks per event until a "per occurrence" limit is reached. For example, an "occurrence may be an earthquake and its after shocks – (may include an Hours Clause' to limit the time period which qualifies as a single occurrence)". Some agreements are on an "aggregate portfolio" rather than a per claim basis (called "aggregate cover excess of loss"). In such cases the liability to pay will be triggered when the total claims for the insurer reach some defined limit during a year.

Non-proportional arrangements are more common in P&C than life insurance, as P&C insurers generally experience greater volatility of claims pattern. In addition, the amount of the claim may be subject to considerable variation, (*i.e.* court settlements), while for life insurance the amount of the claim is generally set out in the policy. Life insurers will generally use proportional reinsurance in order to manage the capital required to support the business written.

The premium may be computed based on the insurer's historic claims experience and what proportion of premium would have been "burned up" by the reinsurance claims (*Burning cost*).

Examples of Reinsurance Types

1. *Proportional Reinsurance Arrangements, Assuming a 40 per cent Risk Reinsurance*

Claim #	1	2	3	4	5
Claim	50 000	75 000	20 000	10 000	30 000
Retention	30 000	45 000	12 000	6 000	18 000
Cession	20 000	30 000	8 000	4 000	12 000

In this case the insurer transfers to the reinsurer 40 per cent of the risks on the policies which it has sold. It will retain the contractual obligations with the insured and will administer the policies.

2. *Excess of Loss Reinsurance, with 20 000 Retention*

Claim #	1	2	3	4	5
Claim	50 000	75 000	10 000	40 000	5 000
Retention	20 000	20 000	10 000	20 000	5 000
Cession	30 000	55 000	–	20 000	–

In this case, the insurer pays any claims up to the limit of retention per risk, 20,000, and the reinsurer pays the balance of the claim. It is settled on a claim by claim basis.

3. *Excess per Risk with 20 000 Retention and Occurrence Limit of 80 000*

Claim #	1	2	3	4	5
Claim	50 000	75 000	10 000	40 000	5 000
Retention	20 000	25 000	10 000	40 000	5 000
Cession	30 000	50 000	–	–	–

In this case, the reinsurer accepts risks on a claim above an excess per risk of 20 000. But if the claims arise from the same event (*e.g.* an earthquake), then the total claim payable by the reinsurer is capped, in this case at 80 000. The reinsurer does not assume any further risk arising from a catastrophic claim. The insurer would need to take out additional reinsurance to cover the possibility of major claims arising from a single catastrophic event.

Financial Goals of Reinsurance

Reinsurance can be used to achieve a variety of financial goals and so plays an important role in facilitating and supporting a sound insurance market capable of assuming a large variety of risks. In particular it can help to diversify and spread risk and so is particularly helpful for smaller companies and markets. However reinsurance contracts can also be used in a variety of situations where there is little transfer of risk, (*i.e.* after claims have been submitted or with predictable lines of business such as life insurance) and then it can be directed at other financial goals, other than pure risk management. Such reinsurance is known as financial reinsurance.

1. Equalisation/Catastrophic Protection

Excess of loss reinsurance reduces the possibility that an insurer will suffer extraordinary losses in a given year. This can be particularly important when there is the possibility of a single event giving rise to significant third party claims, such as an oil spill or damages arising from a civil suit. As such it smoothes income and puts an upper bound on losses, improving the consistency of financial performance over time and providing solvency protection.

2. Surplus Relief

Reinsurance transfers risks and premiums to the reinsurer, effectively reducing the size of the business, thus reducing the amount of capital that is required to maintain a given ratio of risks to capital. Proportional reinsurance can be used to increase surplus when the reserves calculated on transferred risks exceed the true market value of the risks as measured by the reinsurance premium. This will occur when outstanding claims are not discounted in the reserve calculation so that the reserve required for regulatory purposes, (and often tax purposes), over-estimates the true value of the liability assumed by the insurer. The other instance when this arises is when acquisition expenses are not deferred, thus putting a strain on surplus. In these cases the use of reinsurance allows an insurer to sell more business than their own surplus would justify, so maintaining market share or financing a major expansion of their business without acquiring additional capital.

In some cases a regulator may not allow reserves to be reduced if the reinsurer is off-shore and therefore out of its regulatory reach. Some forms of reinsurance (*i.e.* Modco insurance) can deal with this as will be illustrated in an example below.

3. Help Start-up Insurers

Reinsurance allows a start up insurer to effectively borrow surplus for underwriting new business, when marketing capacity exceeds capital available to the firm. The transfer of excess risks of financial loss helps small insurers reduce claims volatility, as they do not have sufficient business to pool risks. The insurer may also be able to make use of the reinsurer's underwriting expertise in order to better price and manage their risks.

4. Source of "Loans"

Reinsurance may be achieved with little or no cash transfer (funds withheld arrangements), and so becomes a type of loan of funds from the reinsurer. It avoids the appearance of debt on the balance sheet and may have tax advantages when interest arising from an ordinary loan would be taxed or subject to restricted deductibility.

5. Avoiding Regulatory Restrictions

In some situations, there may be regulatory restrictions imposed on the insurers to the effect that domestic reserves must be maintained for business which has been ceded offshore. This is intended to maintain the domestic regulator's ability to verify solvency. Rearrangements, known as modified coinsurance (Modco), can be used to circumvent these restrictions.

The following tables illustrate a number of these techniques.

Table 14. **Surplus relief – Non-discounting of outstanding claims**

		Without reinsurance	With reinsurance
1	Premiums received	41.7	41.7
2	Outward reinsurance premium	–	(41.7)
3	Claims incurred reserve	45.0	–
4	Income 1 – (2 or 3)	(3.3)	0
5	Assets	41.7	0
6	Outstanding claims reserve	45.0	0
7	Surplus (5 – 6)	(3.3)	0

Surplus relief (Table 14), called "portfolio loss reinsurance", is generally accomplished by purchasing reinsurance with respect to policies on which claims have already been reported. Thus it is not directed at risk management since there is no underwriting risk – the reinsurer assumes investment risk and some risk relating to the amount of claim to be settled during the runoff of claims. Rather it increases surplus (net assets) because the premium reflects the present value of transferred liabilities while the reserve for the insurer's outstanding claims are based on the ultimate cost and not the discounted value of the claims. Differences can also arise when policy reserves of life insurers do not fully defer acquisition costs or use conservative assumptions in computing the present value. The result is that the policy reserve exceeds the market value of the liability.

The transfer of liabilities on the balance sheet has the effect of increasing income reported on the income statement. Accordingly the insurer can use the technique to smooth out its reported earnings in a year when it has an adverse claims experience. This increases the income of the insurer and could result in an increase in taxation unless the insurer has sufficient tax losses to absorb the increase. If however, the claims are already discounted for tax purposes and acquisition costs are deferred, then the transfer does not have any adverse tax consequences.

Such transactions can also be used to transfer income from taxable insurance companies to those with tax losses and so can be used for selling tax losses. This is known as **reverse surplus relief**.

Under funds withheld coinsurance (Table 15), no cash is transferred to the reinsurer when the premium is due. Instead the insurer establishes a liability on behalf of the reinsurer for the premium (400 above), in effect a loan. This premium due is offset in part by a reinsurance allowance (100) representing the share of the commissions and premium taxes owed by the reinsurer to the insurer with respect to the business that has been ceded The insurer credits interest to the net of these withheld amounts (30). These amounts are combined to leave a net balance outstanding (330). The funds that are withheld are the insurer's liability and the reinsurer's asset (in lieu of cash payments). The reinsurer brings to account the credited interest as investment earnings. The balances in the account are settled periodically or at the end of the contract. Where the reinsurer is credited with a fixed interest rate, the funds withheld are equivalent to coinsurance funded by a loan from the reinsurer. Even though the premium is not paid, it would be reported by the reinsurer as a premium accrued.

Taxing Insurance Companies

Table 15. **Loan – Life coinsurance (funds withheld), 40% reinsurance**

		None	Insurer	Reinsurer
1	Net premiums	1 000	600	400
2	Net Investment return (10% × (1 + 3 − 5))	75	45	30
3	Reinsurance allowances (40% × 5)	–	100	–
4	Net reserve increase	(80)	(48)	(32)
5	Commissions + premium tax	(250)	(250)	(100)
6	Profit (Loss) (1 + 2 + 3 − 4 − 5)	745	447	298
	Balance sheet			
7	Invested assets (1 + 2 − 5)	825	825	–
8	Other assets			330
9	Policy reserves	80	48	32
10	Other liabilities		330	
	Surplus (current year) (6 = 7 + 8 − 9 − 10)	745	447	298

Table 16. **Avoiding regulatory restrictions – Life modco (50% basis)**

		None	Insurer	Reinsurer
1	Net premiums	1 000	500	500
2	Investment return (10% × (1 + 3 + 4 − 7))	50	29	21
3	Reinsurance allowances (50% × 7)	–	250	–
4	Modco adjustment (50% × 5)		40	
5	Net reserve increase	(80)	(80)	
6	Modco adjustment			(40)
7	Commissions + premium tax	(500)	(500)	(250)
8	Profit (loss) (1 + 2 + 3 + 4 − 5 − 7)	470	239	231
	Balance sheet			
9	Invested assets	550	319	231
10	Policy reserves	80	80	–
	Surplus (current year)	470	239	231

With modified coinsurance (Table 16), the insurer retains the reserve and usually the investment risks. It is used when the regulator does not allow the risks associated with business written in its country to be shifted outside of its jurisdiction and control. In this case the regulator requires the insurer to maintain a full reserve for future claims for the risks even though they have been reinsured and so in principle any claims arising from them would be covered by payments from the reinsurer. However the insurer can include in income a modified coinsurance (modco) adjustment equal to the reinsurer's portion of the increase in reserves from writing the policies. The modco adjustment has the effect of transferring to the reinsurer its 50 per cent share of the policy reserve. In the example the adjustment is paid immediately, if the payment were deferred it would include an interest rate applied to the reserves. Where the interest rate is fixed, the insurer retains the investment risk. If the interest rate is the insurer's actual yield on assets, the reinsurer assumes the investment risk. It is similar to a loan from the reinsurer. This can be used to avoid withholding taxes on interest if the interest portion of any eventual payment is not characterised as interest.

Tax Motivations for Reinsurance

As can be seen from the above discussion and examples, there are many non-tax reasons for the use of reinsurance. However, these arrangements can also have a tax motivation, especially when the reserves that are allowed for tax purposes do not accurately reflect the true economic value of the transactions (*i.e.* non-discounting or padded reserves). In some cases, reinsurance may be used for domestic tax planning, in others it may involve international tax planning. Arrangements involving reinsurance include schemes to:

- Transfer losses between taxable and non-taxable insurance companies;
- Transfer assets to a non-resident reinsurer to avoid taxation of the associated investment income;
- Transfer funds to related offshore reinsurers.

Table 17.   **Transfer of losses – 40% quota share**

		None	Insurer	Reinsurer
1	Net earned premium	50.0	30.0	20.0
2	Net Expenses (20% × 1)	20.0	12.0	8.0
3	Net Claims incurred	45.0	27.0	18.0
4	Underwriting profit (1 – 2 – 3)	(15.0)	(9.0)	(6.0)
5	Investment return ((10 %/2) × (100 – 20))	4.0	2.4	1.6
	Profit (4 + 5)	(11.0)	(6.6)	(4.4)

Under quota reinsurance (Table 17) the direct writer pays a reinsurance premium equal to 40 per cent of premiums received to the reinsurer, receives an allowance for expenses and receives payment for the reinsurer's share of claims. The reserve established by the insurer is reduced by the risks that are ceded. In the example, outstanding claims are not discounted and expenses are not deferred. Accordingly the reserve which is allowed for tax purposes exceeds the reinsurance premium which reflects the actual economic cost of acquiring the risks. As profits are computed net of reinsurance ceded to reinsurer this has the effect of transferring losses of 4.4 (40 per cent) to the reinsurer. If the insurer is in a loss position and the reinsurer is taxable then the loss shelters part of reinsurer's income from tax, allowing a reduction in the reinsurance premium charged to the insurer.

If the transaction were made on a funds-withheld basis and the reinsurance premium was paid on settlement with interest, then the transaction would be a form of after-tax financing, since the insurer would receive financing at a reduced rate of interest because of the ability of the lender/reinsurer to shelter other income from tax.

Table 18.   **Transfer of assets – Life coinsurance (50% quota share)**

	None	Insurer	Reinsurer
Net premiums	1 000	500	500
Investment return	50	25	25
Reinsurance allowances		250	
Claims	–	–	–
Net reserve increase	(80)	(40)	(40)
Commissions + premium tax	(500)	(500)	(250)
Acquisition + maintenance	–	–	–
Profit and loss (current year)	470	235	235
Balance sheet			
Invested assets	550	275	275
Policy reserves	80	40	40
Surplus	470	235	235

Coinsurance (Table 18) transfers a proportion of all attributes of the underlying policies to the reinsurer (premiums, expenses, and claims). The scheme can shelter investment income when the reinsurer is offshore. Effectively the offshore reinsurer earns 50 per cent of the investment income. If the reinsurer has been established in a tax haven, the investment income will be able to accumulate on a tax-free basis, once again allowing a reduced reinsurance premium. If the reinsurer is related, then the company has effectively invested the funds offshore to avoid tax.

Policy Options

The principle goal of tax policy in this area should be to restrict the possibility of reinsurance being used to artificially reduce taxes, while maintaining the ability of the insurance industry to use reinsurance for legitimate risk management and other business purposes. Possible responses to tax planning through reinsurance include:

- Treat financial reinsurance as financing;
- Premium tax on offshore reinsurance;
- Restrictions on deductions for re-insurance premiums.

1. *Treat Financial Reinsurance as Financing*

Financial insurance does not transfer significant risk and so can be viewed as a deposit with the reinsurer rather than a true insurance premium. The premium amount is deposited with the reinsurer, investment income accrues with respect to the amount deposited and the original deposit plus an investment return is paid by the reinsurer to the insurer as the claims are settled. Viewed as a deposit the appropriate treatment would be no deduction by the insurer for premiums paid to reinsurer and the interest income would be included in income as it accrues. The reinsurer would not include the premiums in income and would be allowed a deduction for the accrued interest. The insurer would retain the deduction of the full policy reserve.

In order to qualify as true reinsurance, Australia and the US require a transfer of insurance risk (underwriting and timing risk) and exposure to significant loss (computed as the PV of cash flows from a worst case scenario).

Reinsurance transactions must meet the following conditions under the US Anti-Avoidance Rule (IRC 845):

- transfer of insurance (underwriting) risk;
- a business purpose for the reinsurance; and,
- the transactions must not be entered into to avoid tax (if the parties are unrelated) or involve avoidance or evasion if the parties are related (a tougher test) – the related company test requires evidence of significant tax avoidance effects.

A number of characteristics can be used to identify financial reinsurance:

- *Finite risk*: reinsurer's risk of underwriting loss is subject to a limit, this may be effected by clauses such as cancellation provisions, financial guarantees, letters of credit, side agreements, fixed claim schedules or delay of payment clauses;
- *Low risk margin*: reinsurer's expected profit is small and does not follow the fortunes of the insurer; and,
- *Profit commissions*: reinsurer returns excess profits based on a percentage of the reinsurer's net profit (or incurred loss ratio) of the business or with retrospective adjustments, negative experience rated refunds, indemnity commission paid in advance but repayable if the policyholder does not pay the premium (the policy is allowed to lapse), overriding commission over and above the acquisition cost to allow for additional expenses or portfolio commission in additional commission based on the claims experience under a reinsurance treaty.

USA financial reinsurance accounting standards (see FASB Statement No. 113) cover:

- *short-duration* contracts, which include most P&C risks, yearly renewable life insurance contracts and some accident and sickness risks; and,
- *long-duration* contracts which include most life and accident and sickness insurance risks.

Each contract is tested separately (at the inception of the contract) and takes into account side agreements or other contracts that could indemnify the reinsurer. The reinsurer must be subject to the reasonable possibility of beneficial financial loss (not defined). For short-duration contracts there must be a transfer of significant underwriting and investment risk. Long-duration contracts must transfer significant mortality and morbidity risk. Transfer of only investment risk (low return or asset defaults), expense risk (higher than expected expenses), and credit risk (risk that the reinsurer will default on payments), even when significant, is not sufficient to qualify a contract as true reinsurance.

While the basic policy is reasonably clear, discovering instances of financial reinsurance remains a problem during audits, since it is necessary for auditors to review bulky reinsurance agreements to determine the true characteristics of a reinsurance agreement.

2. Reinsurance Premium Tax

Premium taxes generally apply only on premiums paid to the direct writers of insurance. They do not apply to premiums paid to reinsurers under the assumption that the premium has tax has already been paid once by the direct writer. However some jurisdictions (*i.e.* the US) apply premium taxes to premiums paid to non-resident reinsurers. A premium tax on such payments plays the role of a withholding tax in ensuring that the country in which the policy has been written receives a share of the revenue arising from the business. Accordingly countries which levy such a tax may provide exemption through double taxation treaties. A tax on offshore reinsurance premiums may also be seen to play a role in reducing tax avoidance in an area that is hard to audit effectively.

The major argument against premium taxes is that they act as a "tariff" on legitimate reinsurance. Unless the internal market for reinsurance is large and well developed, this will raise the cost of using reinsurance. These extra costs will be passed onto consumers and businesses in the country in the form of higher premiums for insurance and may prevent *bona fide* risk distribution.

The tax would apply to the consideration paid or payable to a reinsurer not licensed to carry on an insurance business in the country. In principle the tax should also apply to certain amounts withheld from the premium by the insurer in order to tax the gross, rather than the net premium. Such amounts would include any "premium reserve" established by the insurer to protect against the reinsurer's default (insurer credits an agreed amount of interest to the fund), and to amounts deducted for reinsurance allowances and profit commissions.

Exemptions for some types of reinsurance are difficult to administer where the premium covers many types of insurance lines of business. The tax should apply to premiums paid by reinsurers and insurance brokers as well in order to prevent them "fronting" tax avoidance. Fronting occurs when an insurer pays a premium to a domestic reinsurer on condition that reinsurer cedes the business to a non-resident (usually related to insurer) or when the insured pays premiums to brokers acting on behalf of non-resident (broker pays premiums to non-resident).

3. Restriction of Deduction of Reinsurance Premiums

Offshore reinsurance could be further discouraged by disallowing a deduction of premiums paid to an offshore reinsurer even if underwriting risk is transferred (Denmark). The arguments for and against this treatment are similar to those for premium taxes, except that the effective rate of tax is much higher when a deduction is denied.

Chapter 8

COMPARISONS OF SELECTED OECD COUNTRIES: TREATMENT OF REINSURANCE[1]

	GENERAL	LIFE
Australia	10% of premiums of reinsurance of Australian risk with non-resident insurer added to taxable income of ceding company. A 3.6% effective tax Exempt from state stamp duties	10% of premiums of reinsurance of Australian risk with non-resident insurer included in taxable income of ceding company (effective rate 3.9%)
Austria	Exempt	Exempt
Belgium	Exempt	Exempt
Canada	Exempt	Exempt
Finland	Exempt	Exempt
Germany	Exempt	Exempt
Ireland	Stamp duty: 0.1% of sum insured	Stamp duty: 0.1% of sum insured
Italy	n.a.	n.a.
Luxembourg	n.a.	n.a.
Mexico	3.5% tax on premiums paid to reinsurers, otherwise exempt	Subject to 10% VAT
Netherlands	Exempt	Exempt
New Zealand	3.8% tax on premiums paid offshore	3.8% of premiums paid offshore
Portugal	Exempt	Exempt
Spain	1.5% withholding tax on non-resident reinsurer on difference between gross amount and commissions and indemnities received from non-resident (no tax if tax treaty)	1.5% withholding tax (exemption through tax treaties)
Sweden	Exempt	Exempt
Switzerland	Exempt	Exempt
United Kingdom	Exempt	Exempt
United States	1% excise tax on premiums paid to non-US reinsurer (may be waived in tax treaties)	Premiums paid to non-US reinsurer (1%) (exemption through tax treaties)

1. Data in tables updated to October 1999.

Chapter 9

LIFE INSURANCE COMPANIES

Nature of Life Insurance

Like P&C insurance, life insurance provides the insurance coverage for policyholders against the risk of loss. However, unlike the risks of financial loss covered under P&C insurance contracts, which relate to loss resulting from theft, accident or natural disasters, life insurance provides cover for the risk to persons of premature death, illness and disability. Thus, life insurance is a form of insurance cover for the loss of potential income resulting from premature death or disability. Life insurance annuities also provide a form of income insurance where benefits are paid to beneficiaries over the remaining life of the beneficiary or beneficiaries. Finally, life insurers also provide more standard investment products such as term annuities which are similar in economic effect to certificates of deposit.

Like P&C insurers, life insurers operate as intermediaries by pooling the premiums and risks of many persons. The insurance risks are transferred to the life insurer which undertakes the underwriting risks if claims experience should be greater than expected. However, unlike most P&C business, the determination of underwriting profit or loss for a life insurer can take many years, due to the long-term nature of many life insurance contracts. Indeed, not until all policyholders die and claims are paid out can a life insurer ascertain its actual underwriting profit. In the case of annual renewable life insurance, the underwriting risks are more similar to P&C insurance and therefore the insurer will be able to quantify its underwriting loss shortly after the end of the contract period.

Life companies may use their actuarial expertise to operate pension businesses. In such cases the pension business is "segregated" from the insurance business in special funds. Also such companies use their investment expertise to provide managed investment funds for individual savers.

Types of Insurance Policies

Life insurers generally provide three distinct types of product: non-life insurance such as accident and health, ordinary life insurance and annuity business.

1. *Non-Life Insurance Policies*

Life insurers in many markets provide forms of non-life insurance related to personal risks. They include the following:

- dental and medical cost insurance;

- long term insurance which is for residential health care, cost of special needs, and a caregiver in the event of long-term incapacity in old age;

- disability insurance which provides periodic benefits in the event of disability resultant from an accident or medical condition which results in the insured person being unable to work;

- dread disease insurance which provides a benefit upon the diagnosis of specified life threatening or debilitating diseases; and

- accidental death which is usually provided as a rider (addition to) another insurance contract for high risk occupations or activities or as a separate travel insurance policy.

2. Ordinary Life Insurance

Ordinary life insurance includes term life insurance, whole life insurance plans, endowment life insurance, and universal life.

Term life insurance policies provide life insurance coverage to the insured person for a fixed period of time. For example, yearly renewable term life insurance, often provided through group insurance plans, provides life insurance for one year. The premiums may be adjusted upon each renewal of the policy. In other cases, the term of the life insurance policy might be five, ten, twenty or more years, with premiums fixed in advance for the term of the contract. One particular term life insurance, term to 100, provides life insurance until age 100 – in effect, it is a whole life plan which does not provide any benefits to the insured other than on death. Some term life insurance policies are renewable on maturity without the insured having to demonstrate their insurability (that is, they do not have to pass a medical examination). The renewal premium is higher due to the policyholder's increased age and the possibility of anti-selection (unhealthy persons will renew). Some term policies are convertible to whole life insurance at any time without evidence of insurability.

Whole life insurance provides life insurance coverage to the insured person for the person's whole life. An important feature of whole life insurance plans, like most life insurance policies, is for premiums to be fixed, and payable over many years. In the case of whole life, premiums are often payable until death or until retirement. As a result, premiums in the early years of a whole life policy greatly exceed the cost of insurance. Therefore, an important difference between term life insurance – particularly term to 100 – is that whole life insurance policies provide two benefits: a benefit on death equal to the sum insured and an amount on termination of the policy prior to death. The amount payable on termination is called the cash surrender value and is usually a portion of the assets, *i.e.* premiums net of expenses, contributed from the date of effect of the policy until termination.

Some whole life policies are *limited pay* policies that restrict the number of payment periods to some fixed number of years. Once all premiums have been paid, the policy is "paid up". Some *adjustable* whole life policies have premiums and/or the sum insured indexed with inflation or asset yields.

Endowment Insurance is similar to whole life insurance in that it builds up capital that is returned to the policyholder and provides life insurance cover over its term. It differs, however, in that it provides for a payment to be made to the policyholder without the surrender of the policy at a fixed date in the future. Therefore it contains an explicit savings function for the policyholder. The fixed payment will often be converted into an annuity at time of maturity.

Universal life insurance takes this process one step further in that it combines two products in a transparent manner – a term insurance product and a savings vehicle. Under universal insurance, the cost of pure insurance and other expenses are deducted from the premium and the balance is kept in an account that earns a market rate of interest. This interest rate may not be fixed in advance, as it implicitly is in other insurance products, in which case the policyholder would accept the investment risk, rather than the insurer.

Some policies may be **participating**, in that they may provide for a basic guaranteed return, with the possibility of further returns if there is a good profit experience with respect to that line of business by the company. Policies that have only a fixed (implicit) rate of return are **non-par policies**.

Savings in Life Insurance Policies

Ordinary life contracts include both an insurance and savings component. The savings component is due to the prefunding of death benefits resulting from the fact that premiums initially exceed benefits on death (death benefit = number of deaths x sum insured). Investment earnings on prefunded premiums contribute to the funding of future benefits. Deferred annuities which provide a fixed flow of income until death also provide a form of insurance coverage.

Pure savings contracts – investment bonds, sinking funds, pure endowment contracts, term certain annuities and some deferred annuities – do not provide insurance pooling. In these cases the main risks accepted by the insurer are investment risks.

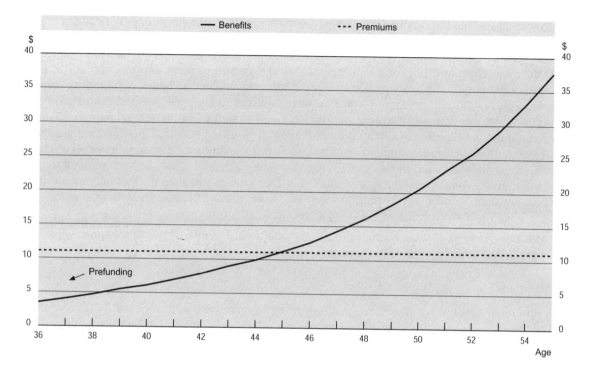

Savings Element of Life Insurance

Prefunding may be returned (net of expenses) when the policy is surrendered (the benefit receivable on lapse of the policy is the *cash surrender value*) for certain types of policies such as whole life.

Annuities

Annuity business is a large portion of the business of a typical insurance company and is comprised of two forms of annuity: immediate annuities and deferred annuities.

1. Immediate Annuities

Immediate annuities provide periodic benefits in return for an up front capital contribution. A *certain annuity* has a fixed number of benefit payments, which will continue to be paid to the survivors of the annuitant in case of death before the termination of the period.

A *straight life annuity* provides benefits until death of the annuitant. If the annuitant dies prematurely, a portion of the capital amount invested is lost. If on the other hand, the annuitant lives longer than expected actuarially, then the payments exceed the capital amount and its accumulated interest. A variant of straight life annuities is a *joint survivor life annuity* that provides benefits until death of the last annuitant on the contract (both spouses).

Some life annuity contracts are a blend of life annuity and certain annuity. For example, a *life income annuity with period certain annuity* provides a guaranteed minimum number of payments while a *refund annuity* guarantees that the benefit payments will return the remaining consideration/capital sum but not interest.

Variable life annuity provides flexible benefit payments based on the investment earnings of a special fund and may or may not have an element of the annuity certain.

2. Deferred Annuities

Deferred annuities are usually pension business and are considered to be life insurance only because the policyholder may purchase a life annuity with the accumulated fund.

Company Taxation – Accounting for Income

Profits in the life insurance business are generally measured in an analogous manner to P&C insurance business. That is, premiums and investment returns are the major sources of taxable revenue of the insurer and commissions, administrative expenses and incurred claims are the major deductions. All premiums are included in income and, in consequence, the insurer establishes reserves against future claims. However there are important differences in the nature of the business and certain of the accounting rules that are normally paralleled in the tax system. On one hand, outstanding claims are usually small and "short-tail" compared with P&C insurance and so such reserves will be relatively small. On the other hand, the incurred claims (*i.e.* the risk has been accepted but has not yet happened) are with respect to events, *i.e.* death, which may not actually occur for many years. Thus the claims which are incurred but not reported form a significant part of the insurer's accrued expenses. Reserves are used to account for these liabilities and these reserves are very large. The size of the reserves relative to income and the number of assumptions which are required in their calculation have traditionally meant that life insurance companies have been very hard to successfully tax, unlike P&C insurance companies.

Some countries – Australia, Ireland, New Zealand, Sweden and the United Kingdom – apply different forms of taxation principally on the net investment income of the life insurer, I-E taxation, which is described in the section on policyholder taxation.

Policy Reserves

As previously indicated, the measurement of a life insurer's profit necessarily involves a long period of time. Profits vary because premiums are low relative to the level of benefits (competition or little claims experience on new business), surrenders are high (insurer does not recover prepaid expenses), mortality is unexpectedly high (*i.e.* AIDS) or investment returns on assets are low.

There are two funding issues for life insurers. On the one hand, the receipt of premiums in excess of current death benefits results in an asset that the insurer must invest to meet future liabilities. On the other hand, a common feature of life insurance policies is that commissions are paid upfront to agents selling the insurance policies. These commissions are usually paid at the time of the insurer accepting to underwrite the policy. For some types of policies these commissions can be two to three times the amount of the premiums received in the first year of the policy.

Thus, in the early years of the policy, the premium in excess of the cost of pure insurance can cover only a part of the expenses, mainly commissions, of the policy. Accordingly, the insurer must use some of its surplus to pay the agent. In a sense, the insurer borrows funds from the policyholder and its shareholders/ participating policyholders so that it can pay for the commission. It expects to recover that surplus with interest through future premium receipts and then to begin to build up capital with respect to the policy.

These two timing issues create difficulties for the computation of the life insurer's policy reserve. The main issues with the policy reserve computation are:

- the treatment of expenses, particularly acquisition expenses;
- the premium used in the reserve computation; and,
- the assumptions used (margin for adverse deviation).

The policy reserve is a measure of the life insurer's future liability with respect to its life insurance policies measured at the end of the current accounting year. This requires a comparison of the present valuation of future liabilities with the present value of future premium receipts. In terms of the benefit and premium components, the life insurer must estimate the probability of death each year under the policy. This is usually easy to do because mortality rates are fairly predictable if the insurer has a sufficiently large pool of policyholders. What is more difficult for the actuary to estimate is the yield the life insurer will earn in the future on the assets it holds to pay future benefits. It is also difficult to estimate the probability that a policyholder will lapse or otherwise terminate its life insurance policy prior to death or the term of the policy. The most basic reserve calculation is the net premium reserve,

$$NPR_t = PV(b) - PV(rp),$$

where b is benefits expected to be paid out in a year and rp is the level premium required to fund those benefits, (that is, it does not include the portion of the premium which is used to fund expenses and to provide a contribution to the surplus of the insurer). The premium, known as the risk premium, is calculated as the level premium that sets the reserve to zero at the beginning of the first year of the policy.

A major issue in the computation of policy reserves is the treatment of acquisition costs. Most ordinary life policies have high acquisition costs in the first year of the policy. Costs later in the policy relate to policy administration costs including payment of benefits, investment and general overhead expenses. The insurer prices the policy to recover the acquisition expenses through the premiums (the premium load for expenses). As noted above, this repayment may take a number of years with multiple premium payment policies.

Under accrual accounting concepts, acquisition costs should be deferred as they represent expenses that relate to the earning of future income, *i.e.* the stream of future premiums. This is accomplished by allowing a full deduction of acquisition costs as they are incurred, but (potentially) offsetting this by taking them into account through the calculation of the policy reserve by netting them in some manner from premiums used for the reserve calculation. The manner in which they are netted gives rise to the principle differences in reserve calculation methods and consequently, to quite different patterns of recognition of profits. In the net premium reserve computed above, the adjustment for acquisition expenses implicitly assumes that they are spread evenly over the premium paying period, since the adjustment for expense loading is the same for each premium. Accordingly, the excess of the premium over the cost of pure insurance in the early years of the policy is treated as if it were available to fund future benefits rather than having been diverted to pay the upfront costs of selling the policy. Thus the policy reserve, which measures the assets set aside to fund future benefits, will be positive even though there are no net assets associated with the policy to be invested.

In many countries, acquisition expenses are deferred, at least partially, through some form of adjustment to the net premium policy reserve defined above. The adjustment can be somewhat arbitrary by using a Zillmerisation approach, which is common in the EC for regulatory purposes. This approach adds expenses (or a portion thereof) to the above reserve computation by treating them as a benefit to the policyholder, therefore relaxing the assumption that all expenses occur evenly over the premium paying period, such that the policy reserve is as follows:

$$PR_t = PV(b + e) - PV(p)$$

Other reserve computations, described below, can be used to adjust the way the reserve is defined.

Different Types of Reserves

There are a number of reserve computations internationally for tax and regulatory purposes. The different techniques used seek to address the major policy issues in the reserve calculation in different ways.

As indicated above the net premium reserve does not defer upfront expenses. The reserve is computed only taking into account death benefits and the receipt of future risk premiums. The reserve at the end of the first year is positive since it reflects the prefunding that has occurred equal to the premium (net of the flat expense loading) plus interest less the cost of pure insurance. (See Column A.)

Column B shows a basic form of Zillermization approach which defers an arbitrary amount of acquisition expenses equal to the first year amount of prefunding – a one year preliminary term reserve. Under this reserving system, there is no reserve at the end of the first year as the excess premiums received have been assumed to be used to fund acquisition expenses.

Column C shows the cash surrender value, that is the amount of the accumulated surplus in the policy after the loan from the surplus of the company used to fund the upfront acquisition costs has been repaid with interest. It represents the amount that the company would be willing to pay to the policyholder should it decide to terminate coverage, (*i.e.* lapse the policy). Ordinarily it will be some percentage of the net assets built up with respect to the policy. Accordingly it reports a zero amount until such time as there is a net positive amount in the policyholder's account.

Under Column D, all forms of benefit and expenses are included in the present value computation of the reserve. This is the policy premium method and it represents the least conservative form of reserving. The policy premium method implicitly recognises the loan from the surplus of the company in the first years of the policy as it accounts for the actual upfront nature of the acquisition costs and the higher premiums in future years that are required to fund them. Accordingly, it can report a negative reserve in the early years of the policy, that is an addition to income, until such time as the "loan" from the surplus of the company has been repaid. This addition to income offsets the immediate deduction that is allowed for the acquisition expenses.

Table 19. **Comparison of life insurance reserves**

Year	A	B	C	D
	Net premium reserve	1 year preliminary term reserve	Cash surrender value	Policy premium reserve
1	5.2	0.0	0.0	(7.8)
2	10.9	5.6	0.0	(4.2)
3	17.0	11.7	0.0	0.4
4	23.6	18.2	0.9	6.0
5	30.7	25.2	2.5	12.3
15	129.2	123.6	74.1	116.1
25	265.3	260.4	234.4	250.4
35	432.8	428.9	386.0	418.8
45	609.4	606.7	546.0	598.8
55	760.3	758.6	682.7	760.7

A major area of controversy in how to calculate reserves for tax purposes is the treatment of margins for adverse deviations (MADs). MADs are adjustments made by actuaries to account for the possibility that future expenses (income) may be higher (lower) than expected in the reserve calculation. It could be argued that the reserve should be calculated using the "best guess" estimates that were used in pricing the policy. This would have the effect of reporting as profit the full expected profit loading of premiums at the beginning of the policy. The actuarial profession would argue that this does not adequately reflect the risks being undertaken by the insurer when it sells the policy. For example, expenses may not be recovered by future premiums due to higher than expected policy lapses. Other adjustments could be to lower the rate of interest credited to the policy reserve below that used for setting the premium or to increase the predicted mortality above the most recent experience, (to anticipate unexpected diseases). However, unexpected events are by no means always negative to the insurer. Advances in medical science and improved lifestyles can reduce mortality rates more than expected. Investment performance can exceed the rate of interest used in the reserve calculation. Accordingly for tax purposes there is a good case that best estimates should be used in calculating the policy reserve. The neutral result would be to allow MADs to the extent that they return the reserve calculated at the beginning of the policy to zero. Since the reserve at the end of the first year is negative, as the upfront costs exceed the first years' premiums, an income inclusion would result which would offset the deduction of the upfront costs. In that case the profits on the policy would be reported over the life of the policy as the insurer is released from risk, that is, to the extent that the actual outcome of the risks assumed by the insurer are better than those assumed in the reserve calculation.

Many countries such as France, Germany, and Portugal define tax reserves to be the same as those reported to the Insurance Regulator. In the case of Canada, the general rule is that the lesser of a reasonable amount and the reserve reported to the regulator is allowed for tax purposes. Other countries such as the USA define the method and assumptions to be used in computing reserves for tax purposes independently from the methods used by the regulators.

Given the prudential nature of regulatory reserves, it would be expected that they already contain a conservative element in their calculation. Accordingly there is a strong case that tax reserves should be less than prudential reserves, and in any case they should certainly not exceed them.

Impact of Different Reserves on Profit

The recognition of profit from life insurance policies is very dependent on the computation of the policy reserve. If acquisition costs are not fully deferred over the premium paying period, losses will result in the initial years of a policy. In a fast growing business, losses on new business will offset profits on policies underwritten in prior years.

Column A shows the net result of the cashflows under the policy. The first year is negative because the acquisition costs exceed premiums. Other expenses and benefits are small in the early years of the policy and so cashflows become positive after the first year. This is the prefunding of the policy, which compensates for the later years when benefits increase and begin to exceed premium income.

The purpose of using reserves is to move from cashflow to accrual accounting. Under the net premium reserve (Column B), acquisition expenses are almost fully deducted in the first year. The entire surplus of the net premium over benefits is treated as a prefunding of future benefits and added to the reserve. Accordingly the cashflow loss recorded in the first year is increased. Overall, the policy reports a loss in present value terms; (this is clearly unreasonable, as the insurer would not enter into contracts on which losses were systematically expected).

The one year preliminary term reserve, Column C, sets the end of first year reserve to zero, effectively deferring that portion of the acquisition expenses which are funded by the excess of the modified net premium over benefits in the first year. However, the "loan" from the surplus of the company is still recorded as a loss, as acquisition costs usually exceed first year premiums. The impact of the preliminary term reserve adjustment is that the loss in the first year is reduced and as a consequence, the policy reports a small profit on a present value basis.

Column D shows the policy premium reserve, taking into account all future income and expenses. It effectively defers all acquisition costs over the policy paying period. In the calculation, margins for adverse deviations have been used to set the reserve to zero as the policy is initiated. In this case the losses experienced in the first years of the other reserving systems are replaced by small profits reflecting the release from risk of the policy. The present value of profit increases substantially compared to the other methods. (If no margins were included, the policy premium method would report all of the future profits *expected* from the policy at the outset of the policy. In this case the present value of income would be higher than shown in the table.)

Table 20. **Impact on profit of life insurance reserves**

	A	B	C	D
	Cash flows (no reserve)	Net premium reserve	1 year preliminary term reserve	Policy premium reserve
Present value		(1.7)	0.8	5.6
1	(6.5)	(11.0)	(6.5)	0.1
2	4.2	(0.1)	(0.7)	0.1
3	4.7	0.3	(0.2)	0.1
4	5.2	0.4	0.0	0.1
5	5.8	0.3	0.0	0.1
15	8.1	2.9	2.5	0.8
25	3.5	3.3	2.9	2.7
35	(3.5)	9.3	8.9	8.7
45	(9.5)	35.6	35.2	35.2
55	134.0	258.9	258.5	258.8

Box 1. **Accounting for income (algebraic approach)**

It is useful to start with the present value of a stream of future amounts $\{X_{t+1}, X_{t+2},...\}$ measured at the end of period "t", assuming that the amount is incurred at the beginning of each period, as follows:

1) $PV_t(X) = [PV_{t-1}(X) - X_t]*(1 + i_t)$

The change in this present value from time "t – 1" to "t" is as follows:

2) $\Delta PV_t(X) = [PV_{t-1}(X) - X_t]*i_t - X_t$

This standard relationship can be used to show the elements of the change in policy reserves. The end of year policy reserve for year t, (R_t), is computed as the present value of expected future benefits and expenses $(PV_t(b + e))$ minus the present value of expected future premiums$(PV_t(p))$, where the present values are computed using an expected rate of interest, i_t, to be credited to the policy for each period

(3) $R_t = PV_t (b + e) - PV_t (p)$

and

(4) $\Delta R_t = \Delta PV_t (b + e) - \Delta PV_t (p)$

$= \{[PV_{t-1}(b + e) - b - e]*i_t - (b - e)\} - \{[PV_{t-1}(p) - p]*i_t - p\}$

$= [R_{t-1} + p - b - e]*i_t + p - b - e$

$= I + p - b - e$

where

$I = [R_{t-1} + p - b - e]* i_t$

The deduction for the increase in policy reserves in computing a life insurer's income can be replaced by (4) above

(5) Income $= P + I - E - B - \Delta R$

$= P + I - E - B - (I + p - b - e)$

$= (P - p) + (I - I) + (b - B) + (e - E)$

where

$I - I$ = the investment return on assets in excess of interest credited to the policy reserve.

$b - B$ = underwriting profit (loss is negative) from death and terminations, to the extent that actual benefit payments, B, are less than expected, b

$e - E$ = expense related profit (loss if negative), to the extent that actual expense payments, E, are less than expected, e

$P - p$ = any other profit included in the premium in excess of the premium used in the policy reserve

Accordingly the amount of income that accrues each period for the policy is equal to the difference between the expected and actual experience under the policy.

Immediate Annuities

There are two possible approaches to the computation of income on financial transactions involving a "deposit" of funds with a financial intermediary. For banks, the receipt of the capital amount of the investment from the annuitant is non-taxable, since the cash received gives rise to an immediate liability on the books of the bank in the form of a deposit. Income is calculated annually as investment revenue on the funds deposited minus the interest credited to the depositor. The life insurance approach is substantially different. The capital sum is treated as a premium and so is subject to tax. To compensate for the fact that the contribution results in a future liability to repay this contribution a policy reserve is calculated. The policy reserve is the present value of future benefits less premiums (in this case nil) using the interest rate and mortality assumptions used in computing the periodic benefits under the policy. Periodic benefits are deductible as they are paid.

If the annuity is a certain annuity and so does not contain an element of insurance, then all amounts can be fixed in advance and the calculation of income under the insurance method will result in the same income flow as with the bank method.

However where not all amounts are fixed in advance, *i.e.* under a life annuity where the payments depend upon mortality, the amounts actually paid can differ from the amounts included in the assumptions used in computing the policy reserve.

Annuities form an important alternative form of investment to ordinary debt instruments and it is important that the interest element of the reserve is reported as interest income and taxed in the hands of the annuitant as it accrues.

Mutual Insurers and Par Policies

Some P&C insurers and life insurers are mutual organisations. Mutual organisations do not have shareholders. Instead, all or a subset of policyholders are the "shareholders" in that they are entitled to share in any distributions by the company of surplus arising from their policies, (the participating policies.) Surplus is accumulated in the participating fund of the company. Where not all policies of policyholders share in the profits of the participating fund, (non-participating policies), profits released from the non-participating fund may be shown as surplus of the insurer.

Stock companies with participating funds are sometimes limited to the amount of profits that can be transferred annually to the shareholders' account (90-97.5 % in Canada depending on the fund's size).

The premium of a participating policy includes a contribution to the insurer's capital. The extra premium is the present value of future expected policy dividends and bonuses (similar to a share price computation)

Profits of participating policies are distributed by:

- policy dividends, refunds or rebates of premiums;
- terminal bonuses added to the sum insured on death or surrender, or maturity of the policy;
- reversionary bonuses which provide a guaranteed addition to the sum insured when the bonus is declared.

The declaration of these profit distributions results in an increase in policy reserves which are computed assuming (implicitly or explicitly) that expected future dividends and bonuses are a policy benefit. Terminal bonuses and reversionary bonuses increase the policy reserve by increasing the sum insured and therefore future policy benefits paid out as claims on death.

Dividends and capital gains on the capital portion of the premium may not be taxed in the hands of the policyholder. For example an increase in death benefits by way of reversionary bonuses are not taxed assuming that death benefits are not taxable. Policy dividends may be treated as a return of premiums and not taxable if the premium was non-deductible. Belgium and US, on the other hand, attempt to impute a return of capital to policyholders.

International Taxation Issues

Some countries do not tax world-wide income of life insurers. This can be another source of difficulty in taxing insurance companies. In some cases there may be a *general exemption* from domestic tax on income of foreign branches regardless of type of business (France), or in the case of insurance companies there may be an exemption under the *mutuality principle*. Under that principle, profits of mutual insurers on foreign branch income are exempt on the basis that surplus belongs to foreign policyholders (the USA applies the principal for policies sold in Mexico and Canada). Another reason cited why life insurance companies are not subject to tax on world-wide taxation is the fact that life insurers are subject to very different forms of tax internationally. As a result of this variance, the general approach of taxing world-wide income with a credit for foreign taxes paid may not work well. Finally, insurers will argue that world-wide taxation will disadvantage them in foreign markets where local companies are subject to lower taxation. Since there are commercial advantages of using branches (perceived higher capitalisation securing the policies), insurers, like banks may use branches rather than subsidiaries and so be exposed to immediate domestic taxation in the absence of the exemption. An exemption for foreign branches requires difficult branch accounting allocation rules.

Problems also arise in other systems, such as the I-E system in the UK which seeks to apply the I-E system to domestic business only, but applies more ordinary principles to offshore business. Moreover the application of domestic tax to the local branches of non-resident insurers raises similar difficulties.

1. Non-residents

Where non-residents establish branches to sell policies in a jurisdiction it is necessary to establish rules to determine the source of income and expenses. In particular:

Profit margins are small expressed as a proportion of assets *(e.g.,* 1.5%). Any error in allocation can result in a significant reduction or elimination of tax payable.

Box 2. Determining Source of Income and Expenses

Premiums	Residency of policyholder or where the insurer is carrying on a business
Investment return	Factual determination based on financial statements may be of little help due to consolidation of accounts and solvency computed in home country (problem in EC)
Expenses	Factual allocation
Claims/benefits	Residency of policyholder or where the insurer is carrying on a business
Policy reserves	Residency of policyholder or where the insurer is carrying on a business

---

2. Determining investment income of a branch

Investment income of non-residents with a domestic branch needs to be computed on a factual basis or using a formula. These rules may also apply to resident multinationals if they are exempt from domestic tax on income from overseas branches. Canada, the UK and the USA use branch accounting with special rules for determining investment revenues and interest costs. These rules stipulate a minimum level of assets for tax purposes and a minimum return on those assets. The company then designates assets with respect to its business in the jurisdiction in a manner that is consistent with these constraints.

In the US and Canada, minimum assets are computed as:

• policyholder related liabilities connected to the branch (based on residency of policyholder but may also include other policies if underwritten from that branch);

• deemed minimum capital and surplus (based on minimum regulatory requirements or the average the total world-wide capital and surplus of the insurer).

An average of prior accounting year and current accounting year "deemed" assets is computed. Canada does not use a simple average. Under proposed legislation applicable from 1999, Canada uses a weighted-average based on monthly cash flows. Assets are then designated to fill the basket of assets.

Canada and US also have a minimum yield on assets rules. Canada determines the order in which investment assets may be used to fulfil the required total amount. That is, investments with the lowest tax effort are the last to be allocated to the business to determine investment income.

Overseas branches of UK companies designate assets in the following order:

- assets solely linked to overseas liabilities;
- non-linked assets that are foreign currency assets;
- assets under the control of the overseas branch;
- government securities issued with the condition that they are free of tax to non-residents;
- assets other than shares in UK companies;
- shares in UK companies.

Gains may be taxed when assets are transferred out of the branch. No deduction may be claimed if transferred assets have losses (until the asset is sold). Allocation of debt and interest expenses is problematic. The US uses a fungibility approach. The US limits the interest deduction to the total interest expenses of the company times the ratio of US liabilities to Worldwide liabilities. Austria, and Switzerland prorate worldwide profits of non-residents using formulae based upon liabilities in the different jurisdictions.

Chapter 10

COMPARISONS OF SELECTED OECD COUNTRIES: INCOME TAXES ON LIFE INSURERS[1]

	Basis of taxation	Life insurance provisions	Securities
Australia	I-E tax 39% for mutual life companies; 36% for other life companies; 33% for friendly societies on eligible insurance business 39% for accident and disability component		Revenue account on disposition of securities
Austria	34% of accounting profits with exceptions	Reserve computed using conservative interest rate, mortality assumptions – reserve cannot exceed cash surrender value	Revenue treatment on disposition of securities (write down investment if market value < cost)
Belgium	40.2% of accounting profits with exceptions	Cash surrender value of policy which may be less than liability in profit and loss account	Capital gains on shares are exempt
Canada	38-46% of taxable income, (varies by province)	Regulatory reserves as of 1996	Revenue account. Shares marked to market as of 1995 and realised gains on debts securities amortised over remaining term to maturity
Finland	28% of accounting profits with exceptions	n.a.	Revenue treatment and asset appreciation taxed as revenue
Germany	40% of accounting profits with exceptions	Zillmerized reserves as defined	Revenue treatment on dispositions of securities (write down investment if market value < cost
Ireland	28% I-E tax		Revenue treatment on dispositions of securities and unrealised gains if part of trading profit
Italy	37%		n.a.
Luxembourg	30% of accounting profits with exceptions		Revenue treatment on disposition of securities
Mexico	35% of accounting profits	Tax deductible allowance	Ordinary corporate income tax for realised gains on securities
Netherlands	35% of accounting profits with exceptions	Net level premium reserve using interest rate and mortality assumptions used in premium setting – conservative reserve since no deferral of acquisition costs	n.a.
New Zealand	33% I + U – E tax where U: (1. mortality profit, 2. premium loading, 3. profit on surrenders)	None	Revenue treatment on disposition of securities. Life assurers assessed capital gains.

1. Data in tables updated to October 1999.

	Basis of taxation	Life insurance provisions	Securities
Portugal	37.4% of accounting profits with exceptions	Defined by Portuguese Insurance Institute	Revenue treatment on disposition of securities
Spain	35%, mutuals 25%, co-ops 20% of accounting profits with exceptions	n.a.	Revenue treatment on disposition of securities
Sweden	27% I-E on E insurance (15% on P-insurance)		n.a.
Switzerland	35% (varies by Canton) of accounting profits		
United Kingdom	30% I-E tax. Pensions 0%		Revenue or capital gains treatment on disposition of securities
USA	35% tax on profits under Internal Revenue Code	As defined using conservative mortality and interest rate assumptions – some portion of acquisition costs deferred	Revenue treatment on disposition of securities – some securities may be marked to market

Chapter 11

TAXATION OF POLICYHOLDERS

While the focus of this paper is on the taxation of insurance companies, the taxation of the companies is closely related to the taxation of policyholders and so this section briefly explores some of the issues that are raised in the context of policyholder taxation.[1] It should be emphasised that the focus is on life insurance policies which are not considered to be part of the pension regime of a country and, accordingly, which should be subject to ordinary accrual taxation. Private pensions, which are often offered through insurance companies, are generally subject to a preferential regime of deferred taxation and are not covered in this study.

Introduction

The taxation of policyholders raises four basic questions. In general, countries have answered these questions in many different ways, depending upon their general treatment of income from savings, the relationship of their insurance system to their provision of pensions and the more general social policy context, for example in the area of health care. These are:

- treatment of premiums paid by individuals;

- treatment of disbursements arising from the policy;

- treatment of premiums paid by employers; and,

- treatment of income which accrues over the life of the policy.

In theory the treatment of these categories are interdependent and should be internally consistent. It is not possible to say categorically what the treatment of benefits should be without knowing whether or not premiums paid were deductible. Even within the taxation of benefits, failure to apply first best taxation will lead to second best answers that are different for various categories of benefits. Country taxation varies widely, and is often internally inconsistent as it has developed in an *ad hoc* manner without relying on an overarching consistent framework.

Tax Treatment of Premiums Paid by Individuals

The treatment of premium payments paid by individual policyholders varies widely among OECD countries. According to income taxation principles, individual taxpayers should not be entitled to deduct insurance premiums in computing taxable income, as the purchase of insurance is a form of consumption of protection from catastrophic loss or, depending on the type of policy, a form of savings. This is the treatment in countries such as the US and Canada. However in a number of countries, particularly in Europe, premiums paid on ordinary life insurance may be deductible, at least up to certain limits. The reason for this is that life insurance is seen as part of the pension and social support system, and therefore socially desirable. Such deductibility provides an explicit incentive for this form of savings.

---

1. For a more general treatment of issues involving the taxation of savings see Taxation and Household Savings, OECD 1994.

Tax Treatment of Benefits Paid to Individuals

The tax treatment of benefits from life insurance policies also varies greatly across countries. Moreover life insurance policies pay benefits to policyholders in a number of ways and there may be inconsistencies in taxation within a country depending upon the manner in which the benefit is paid. Benefits can be seen as arising from three sources:

- from the return of premiums paid;
- from the effect of pooling of the pure insurance portion of the premium; and,
- an increase in the value of the benefit over the premium paid due to income earned on the savings component of the premium.

In theory the treatment of the benefits arising from pure insurance should complement the treatment of the premiums. If premiums are deductible, then the benefits should be taxable as both the returned premium and the pooling benefits are being paid out of proceeds which have previously been deductible. On the other hand, if the premiums were not originally deductible then the insurance part of the benefits should not be taxable income as the benefit simply covers the loss which gave rise to the payment.

Any benefits arising from a return earned on the saving component of the premium should give rise to some form of taxation whether or not the premiums had been deductible. As discussed below the return to savings, (the principal part of the premium in excess of administrative costs, the cost of pure insurance and the profit portion of the premium), should be taxed as it accrues, (a result that occurs in a minority of OECD countries). In some countries, certain forms of benefit are taxed when they are paid, a form of deferred taxation of the accrued inside build up. And if the premiums were deductible, then, under an income tax, both the inside build up *and* the benefit paid should be taxable in order to remove the deferral benefits implicit in the original deduction. In fact in many countries, neither the inside build up nor the final benefit payment are taxed. This is a source of significant tax benefit and can lead to the tailoring of insurance products as savings vehicles with a consequent avoidance of tax on investment income. For this reason a number of countries which formerly allowed deductions for premiums paid have eliminated or curtailed this relief recently.

What is a benefit, when is it taxed and what is its value? These are questions that also give rise to a wide variety of approaches. Methods of paying benefits include:

- *Lump sum payments* – typically death benefits or one-off payments which qualify for compensation. Should be taxed as outlined above, but in fact, death benefits are rarely subject to taxation for social policy reasons and due to the obvious political difficulty in doing so.

- *Periodic payments* – may be immediate as with disability pensions or deferred, generally as part of a pension scheme. One treatment would be to tax the capital value of the benefit as with an ordinary lump sum payment, and then treat the periodic payments as with an annuity, where the interest portion of the payment would be taxed and the principal portion would be tax free. However in many circumstances such as disability pensions the payments are considered to be for income replacement and so are taxable. Arguably then, the premiums paid for such insurance should be deductible.

- *Cash surrender* – with whole life and endowment policies, a part of premiums are set aside each year to fund future benefits and form a reserve of cash accumulating in the policy. A percentage of such amounts may be payable to the policyholder on surrender of the policy. If investment income has been taxed on the policy as it accrues then no further tax is necessary, assuming that premiums have not been deductible. If not then the accumulated income can be taxed by comparing the amount received with the cost of the policy, (premiums net of costs, benefits previously paid and insurance purchased.

- *Policy dividends* – are payments with respect to participating policies which return a portion of the cash accumulation within a policy to the extent that it exceeds that which is necessary to fund future benefits. In some countries industry has successfully argued that the dividends are a return of (non-deductible) premiums and do not represent income unless they drive the cost of the policy below zero. This would be like arguing that no income results on a interest bearing investment until the total interest payments exceed the principal invested, and results in a deferral of tax. However, if inside build up is taxed and there has been no deduction for premiums, then policy dividends would simply be a return of previously taxed income and would not be subject to tax.

- *Increases in coverage of policies* – higher than expected returns on a policy may allow a company to increase the coverage of the policy as a form of benefit. This is analogous to paying a lump sum benefit to the policy holder and then selling more coverage on the policy and should be taxed as such.

- *Policy loans* – are loans made to a policyholder out of the funds that are accumulated in a policy. They allow the policyholder temporary access to capital without diminishing their insurance coverage. Assuming that they are repayable and bear a market rate of interest and that the interest is taxable as part of the inside build up of the policy they do not give rise to a taxable benefit. If the interest rate were less than the market rate of interest then the difference between it and a market rate of interest should be taxable.

Tax Treatment of Employer-paid Premiums

The treatment of employer paid premiums depends upon who is the beneficiary, the employer or the employee(s). In the first case the employer purchases protection for the death of a key employee or a partner (*i.e.* to purchase back the partnership interest of the partner). In the second the employer purchases insurance as part of a benefit package for its employees. In either case, the employer should deduct the premiums on policies written as a business expense. If the employer receives the benefit, it should be taxable.

When the employee is the beneficiary, the premium should be taxable in the hands of the employee as a form of fringe benefit. (Generally the fringe benefit is measured by the premium paid, which is related to the amount of insurance purchased, rather than the benefit, which is a compensation for a loss which has been incurred. This is the appropriate result unless there is a form of avoidance through disguised wages where the value of the benefits exceed the premiums paid.)

Some group insurance plans are partly (or wholly) funded by employer-paid premiums. The employer is the policyholder. Premiums paid by the employer are deductible as a business expense. Premium refunds and dividends paid to the employer should be taxable revenue. Employer-paid premiums should be a taxable benefit to the employee. The benefit to individual employees can be measured by their share of total coverage under the plan divided by the premium paid. Some countries do not tax such fringe benefits on group term insurance up to some limit of coverage per employee, in order to encourage such plans for social policy reasons. (For example, in the United States given the absence of general government-supported health care. Life and health insurance fringe benefits related to pure insurance (term insurance) paid to the employee (and their dependants) under the plan would not be taxable up to a limit of coverage per employee.) Employee-paid premiums are, in principle, not deductible, and of course do not give rise to a taxable benefit.

Group plans typically are of a one year duration. Insurance companies would generally expect to be able to predict quite accurately the total number of claims from each policy due to the law of large numbers. However they are exposed to a termination risk to the extent that they have an abnormally high number of claims in a year, and then the policy is not renewed by the employer. To guard against this problem, they will often set aside a portion of a premium in a reserve to allow for experience-rated refunds to be paid to the employer after a period of time which allows them to better estimate the occurrence of claims for a given plan. This situation can give rise to tax deferral if such refunds are accumulated but not paid. In that case investment income may accrue on the excess premiums which is not taxed in the hands of the employer, because the refund has not been paid, and which is not taxed in the hands of the insurance company because it is sheltered by a reserve. To prevent this, income accrued

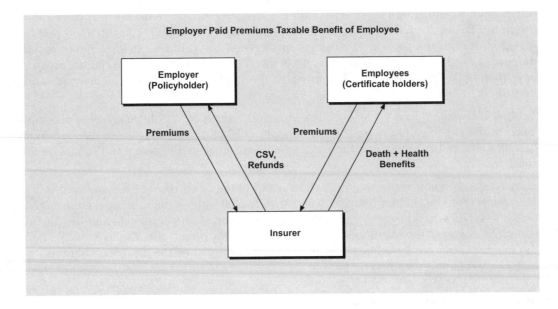

with respect to reserves for experience rated refunds should be taxed in the hands of the plan holder, the employer, as it accrues.

Inside Build up

Inside build up is the investment return credited to policyholders that is a result of the payment of premiums in excess of the current insurance claims and other costs of the insurer – that is, due to the prefunding of future benefits. The insurer invests the cash received from premium payments in investments usually matched to the nature of the liability. Long term liabilities are matched with long term assets.

The investment income earned on these assets is not taxed in the hands of the insurer to the extent that it is used to fund future benefits, as that amount of income is effectively sheltered from tax by the year over year change in the policy reserve. This is appropriate as the income accrues to the benefit of the policyholder. However it is also appropriate that the income be taxed on behalf of the policyholder in some manner. This happens in some but not all jurisdictions and in a number of different ways.

Under investment bonds and deferred annuity contracts the insurer will credit the policyholder with an *explicit* investment return on the deposit (or capital sum) net of expenses. These amounts should be subject to tax directly in the hands of the policyholder.

However, the savings component in ordinary life insurance policies earns an *implicit return*. The insurer implicitly guarantees the policyholder a *certain* investment return by taking into account expected investment returns in computing premiums. The savings component is substantial in whole life plans which provide a cash surrender value to return a portion of the inside build up on termination of the policy and may be a principal motive for purchasing endowment plans. However, term life insurance contracts (without a CSV) can also have sizeable inside build up due to the prefunding of benefits if their period of coverage is sufficient.

Universal life insurance plans make the inside build up explicit as they separately identify the savings component. The policy separates the net cost of insurance (the term insurance premium) from investment income and expenses.

Methods of Inside Build-up Taxation

There are two general alternatives for taxing the inside build up

- tax the policyholder;
- tax the insurer.

The policyholder can be taxed

- annually on the interest credited to the cash surrender value of the policy (Norway);
- only when the policy is surrendered and the policyholder receives cash (USA).

Taxing the policyholder on income as it accrues is the theoretically correct approach. This provides a taxation result which is equivalent to the regime which applies to other savings vehicles as the income is taxed as it is earned and at the rate which is appropriate to the individual policyholder. Using the cash surrender value, as does Norway, may not tax all of the inside build up as not all of the investment income which is accrued to fund future death benefits may be allocated for cash surrender. In the case where tax is applied only when the policy is surrendered, a deferral of tax results relative to the accrual taxation of the income. Moreover, if taxes are paid only on surrender, and not on claims, an outright relief from taxation occurs. While theory would suggest that taxation of surrender should be extended to death benefits, the political problems with doing this are self-evident. Taxing the policyholder also gives rise to complexity as amounts for each policy must be reported to individual policyholders who will neither have a cashflow to fund payment of tax nor are they likely to understand the nature of the income being earned under the policy. For these reasons it may be preferable to levy the tax on the investment income in the hands of the insurer as a form of simplification.

The life insurer can be taxed in lieu of taxing the policyholder in a number of ways. Examples are:

- I-E tax (UK, Australia);
- I-E+U (New Zealand);
- Investment income tax (Canada);
- Real interest rate tax (Denmark).

A principal issue with this form of taxation is to choose the tax rate. Ideally it would be set equal to the tax rate applying on investment income of individuals. The problem is that, with a progressive personal income tax system, different individuals face different marginal tax rates. If the rate on investment income is set too low, then high-income taxpayers receive a benefit and the possibility of tailored tax avoidance vehicles still remains, (particularly if the top marginal tax rate is high). If the tax rate is too high, then lower income policy holders are disadvantaged.

1. Measuring the Inside Build up in the CSV

Whole life insurance policies include a cash surrender value on termination of the policy (other than by death) because of the prefunding of future benefits. The premium includes this benefit and therefore the premium is higher than a comparable term to age 100 policy where there is no CSV. The CSV is a measure of the policyholder's share of assets (a *portion* of cumulative cash flows from policy inception)

CSV = x % * (premiums + interest – net cost of insurance – expenses – dividends and bonuses)

Inside build up on termination =

CSV – Cost of the policy = total interest – total expenses credited to the CSV

Cost of the policy = premiums paid – dividends – net cost of insurance

The US does not reduce the cost of the policy by the net cost of insurance. Canada does. Annual inside build up can be measured as

Annual inside build up = change in CSV – change in cost of the policy = Income – Expenses in the year

2. The I-E Tax (UK)

The UK and Australia do not attempt to separate the income of the company and the policyholder and tax them separately. Instead they tax all of the investment income accruing to life insurance policies and it is intended to tax both the inside build up and investment profits of the life insurer. This has the advantage that it avoids the need to compute policy reserves. A number of adjustments are made to income and expenses. Investment income is net of franked dividends. Management costs of acquisition are spread over a fixed 7 year period – including for term insurance policies of less than 7 years. Miscellaneous sources of income, such as securities underwriting fees, are added to the tax base. Capital gains (CG) on disposition of shares and real property are added to the tax base, as they are not considered to be income in the UK.

Underwriting profits are not subject to the tax. The I-E tax does not attempt to remove underwriting related expenses. The insurer deducts both investment-related expenses and underwriting expenses against its investment income.

While the problems of the policy reserves are avoided serious tax planning problems remain with the I-E tax.

a) Allocation Issues (I-E Tax)

Less than 40% of business is subject to I-E tax. There are serious allocation issues in trying to exclude certain businesses from the I-E tax.

Basic Life Assurance and General Annuity Business (BLAGAB) are subject to the I-E tax. Pension business, business conducted in overseas branches are taxed on the profit from that business as reported to the Insurance Regulator rather than through the I-E tax. It would not have been appropriate to levy tax on pension products sold through life offices if other pension products are not subject to taxation. Investment income of exempt business is generally removed through a formula, *i.e.*, based on average assets or average liabilities attributable to the business.

For overseas business, assets are determined by adding overseas liabilities and appropriate assets and designating assets in a certain order (see Life Insurance: Company Taxation)

A factual method of allocating investment income may lead to the insurer removing the highest yield assets from that associated with the taxable business in order to reduce taxes payable. On the other hand, a formulary approach allocates the average return and surplus across all business, which may not be appropriate, based on commercial requirements

b) Reinsurance tax planning (I-E Tax)

I-E tax was subject to significant tax planning through the use of reinsurance. By design the tax was net of reinsurance. Actual investment income and actual management expenses of an insurer (and reinsurer) were subject to I-E tax. In response, offshore reinsurance was used to:

- export "I" by transferring assets offshore;
- import "E" through yearly renewable term insurance.

Inland Revenue has indicated that more than 1 billion pounds sterling of tax revenue was lost with the reinsurance of single premium policies.

- the policies were reinsured overseas using modified coinsurance;
- profit was returned to the UK insurer through profit allowances and experience refunds which are not assessable as miscellaneous revenue under the I-E tax.

Yearly Renewable Term reinsurance of foreign policies imported expenses (reinsurance allowance for cedant's costs) but virtually no interest income as this is pure insurance underwriting (I = 0, E = reinsurance allowance). The solution was that reinsurers are now subject to profit tax (not I-E tax). Insurers must increase investment income for reinsurance ceded. I-E tax is now "gross of reinsurance" on the basis that policyholder tax should be independent of reinsurance.

3. New Zealand I + U-E Tax and Policyholder Tax

New Zealand applies two levels of tax at the life insurance company level which are intended to tax the income of the company and the income of the policyholder in a consistent manner. The I-E+U tax is directed at the income of the life insurer. A separate policyholder tax, which is collected by proxy at the company level, is levied on the inside build-up. Tax collected under the company tax on the inside build up is creditable against the policyholder tax.

The I-E + U tax is applied to the inside build-up plus the insurer's profit from investment and underwriting. As such it extends the traditional I-E tax to other sources of profit to the insurance company and so avoids the problem of (non-)allocation of expenses associated with the two sources. The underwriting profits arise from two sources:

- profit on mortality and termination risks;
- premium load (to reflect underwriting expenses) deemed to be 20% of the net cost of pure insurance for life insurance and 1% of reserves released on death in the case of life annuities.

The latter adjustment removes the underwriting expenses in an arbitrary manner and does not lead to an exact matching of income and expenses. Gains on sale of shares and property (generally exempt under the income tax in New Zealand) are included in I-E + U.

New Zealand also applies taxation at the basic individual tax rate to the inside build up on a policy accruing to the individual policyholder. In order to simplify compliance, the tax is paid by the company. The inside build-up is measured using an additive formula equal to the Increase in Reserves plus Benefits plus Underwriting Profits minus Premiums. The full deduction of premiums provides up-front relief for investment related expenses, therefore there is mismatching. The tax base is increased by (1 – the policyholder level tax rate) to arrive at the before tax amount necessary to provide the after-tax benefit implicit in the policy. A tax credit is given to the extent that the inside build up has already been taxed at the company level under the I-E+U tax.

4. Canada's Company Tax on Inside Build-up

Canada has resorted to a simple formula approach to tax the inside build up earned by the company on behalf of policyholders – the Investment Income Tax (IIT). The IIT is levied at a rate of 15% of a life insurer's taxable Canadian investment income. In determining a life insurer's taxable investment income, the tax applies an average notional net of expense interest rate to the mean reserves of taxable policies (55% * notional interest rate * mean reserves gross of reinsurance). The formula attempts to remove underwriting expenses and match expenses with investment return by assuming that capitalised expenses are 45% of the interest rate. To avoid double taxation, the insurer deducts inside build-up that policyholders are taxable on directly. (In fact to the extent that reserves are already net of expenses no adjustment for underwriting expenses are necessary. In that case the principle question is what is the appropriate interest rate to use to calculate the benefit. While in principle, this rate will vary by policy, attempts to fine tune such a formula are likely to be complex and a major source of error and avoidance.)

Chapter 12

COMPARISONS OF SELECTED OECD COUNTRIES: POLICYHOLDER TAXATION[1]

	Premiums	Employer paid premiums	Benefits	inside-build-up
Australia	Not deductible	Non taxable benefit	Non taxable unless policy held < 10 yr. – net proceeds taxed – rebate for I-E tax paid by life office	I-E tax
Austria	25% of premiums deductible from income up to a max. of ATS 10 000/yr (only for straight life annuity); add amounts for single earner and children; reduced/no deductibility for income>500 000/70 000; pension contributions and special life insurance products; a certain percentage of premiums paid (up to a maximum amount depending on the average yield of bonds) is deductible from income tax.	No taxable benefit up to a limit of 4 000 ATS/ employee per year	Benefits paid at once(endowment insurance): taxable if single premium policy held < 10 yr (difference between benefits and total premiums paid) Annuities: taxable after the sum of received annuities exceeds its present value as defined in tax law; Pension contributions and special life insurance products: benefits not taxable	Taxation of the difference between deducted premiums and surrender benefit in the case of: surrender within 20 yr in case of endowment insurance; • changes of annuities to benefit at once or surrender of annuities. • Taxation of deducted premiums with flat rate of 30% In case of pensions contributions and special life insurance products: repayment of deducted income premiums
Belgium	Life premiums non-deductible, however, tax credit of 30% to 40% (limit 15% of first BF 56 000 plus 6% of balance up to BF 67 000). Pension contributions deductible up to BF 22 000 (single person)	Non taxable benefit	Benefit taxed at 10% – tax levied at age 60. Pension benefits taxable unless paid on retirement or at age 65 in which case subject to 16.5%.	Taxed as part of benefit
Canada	Not deductible	Taxable benefit	Benefits non taxable	Annuities and "savings oriented" life insurance policies taxed annually in hands of policy holder. At the insurer level, other life insurance policies are subject to a 15% tax levied on net interest income credited to life insurance reserves (*i.e.,* 15% of [(0.55% of an interest rate earned on mean reserves) – amounts credited to policyholders])
Finland	Not deductible	Taxable benefit	Yield taxable capital benefit on expire/ surrender at 29%	Exempt

1. Data in tables updated to October 1999.

	Premiums	Employer paid premiums	Benefits	inside-build-up
Germany	Deductible up to limits, if policy held min 12 yr. – Limit reduced by social security contributions	Taxable benefit	Benefits taxable depending on age Premium deduction reversed if policy held < 12 yr.	If contributions to life insurance can (in principle) be deducted, the accruing interest is also tax exempt. If the benefit is paid out as a lump-sum, there is no taxation. In the case of annuity payments, the interest accruing after the first payment is subject to tax.
Ireland	Not deductible		Benefits not taxable except if proceeds received by other than original beneficiary or if contributions paid *and* deducted by employer	I-E tax
Italy	19% tax credit (max. L2 500 000) if held min. 5 years	Non taxable benefit	Benefits non taxable	None
Luxembourg	Deductible max. of LUF 18 000 (single person)		Benefits non taxable	Exempt
Mexico	Insurance premiums are not deductible except for pension contributions	Deductible for the employer	1. Benefits exempt 2. Pension benefits taxable at retirement	1. Roll-up exempt if the premiums were paid by the insured. 2. Roll-up partially or totally taxed if the premiums were paid totally or partially by the employer
Netherlands	Generally non-deductible	Non taxable benefit	Benefits non-taxable	Exempt
New Zealand	Not deductible	Taxable benefit	Benefits non taxable	Actuarial formula (change in reserves + benefits – premiums + underwriting adjustments/[1 – policyholder tax rate]). Tax credit given for taxes paid by life office under I + U-E tax
Portugal	Fiscal benefits	Fiscal benefits	Exempt	n.a.
Spain	Pension: contributions deductible (lesser of 20% of salary income and 1 100 000 pesetas)	Taxable benefit	Death benefits taxable. Annuity benefits taxed at rate based on recipient's age (<40 yr. 45%; < 50 yr. 40%; <60 yr. 35%; <70 yr. 25% and >70 yr. 20%). Wealth tax applies on cash value, benefits subject to inheritance tax	As part of benefit

	Premiums	Employer paid premiums	Benefits	inside-build-up
Sweden	E-insurance (life and endowment) premiums non deductible P-insurance (pension contributions) premiums deductible equal to the greater of 5% of salary income and SEK 18 300 – maximum deduction is 36 600.	n.a.	Income received from pension insurance taxable income	30% tax on investment income of E-insurance (endowment). 10% tax on investment income of P-insurance (pension)
Switzerland	Deductible	n.a.	Benefits subject to tax if it is capital insurance used for old age security	As part of benefit if taxed
United Kingdom	Life premiums not deductible Pension contributions deductible up to 17.5-40% of earned income depending on age	Non taxable benefit up to 17.5-40% of earned income depending on age	Benefits of qualifying policies non taxable. Non-qualifying policies subject to higher rate top-up charge of 17%	I-E tax Interest element of life annuities taxable
USA	Not deductible	Taxable benefit	Benefits non taxable	Exempt if not savings product otherwise subject to accrual taxation

1. Life insurance premiums only, does not include private pension contributions.

Chapter 13

ALTERNATIVE METHODS OF TAXING FINANCIAL INSTITUTIONS

Designing and administering effective income taxation systems for insurance companies, especially life companies, can be very difficult. These difficulties arise for a number of reasons.

First is the complexity of the operations of the industry. Calculations of reserves necessarily rely on a series of assumptions. Given the conservatism inherent in actuarial calculations, reserve calculations may lead to a deferral of tax. Moreover, with the advent of new financial instruments, the products used for investment have become more complicated and further avenues for tax avoidance have been opened up.

Second is the increasing internationalisation of the business. Whether in trying to tax the domestic income of residents with operations offshore, or in trying to tax the subsidiaries or branches of non-residents, determining the source of income and expenses can be difficult. These problems are exacerbated by the existence of low-tax offshore financial regimes that attract taxable income away from normal tax regimes.

Third many avenues for after-tax financing make use of financial intermediaries as the recipients for the unutilisable losses of others. While the benefits of such schemes usually accrue principally to the loss making firms, it is the tax of the financial institution that is foregone by the government.

Finally, financial institutions often operate on very low margins. Income is a small residual when costs are subtracted from revenues. Therefor small percentage deviations in either revenue or costs can have a significant impact on income.

Because of these reasons, a number of countries have instituted alternative taxes on insurance companies and other financial institutions in order to ensure that the sector contributes some tax.

Issues

There are a number of considerations in assessing whether or not to introduce an alternative tax. In many cases these considerations lead in conflicting policy directions and so trade-offs are inherently necessary.

a) Securing revenues

First and foremost, the goal of an alternative tax is to raise revenues. Insurance companies can be very profitable and it is reasonable that they should make an appropriate contribution to national tax revenues. Ideally this should be done through a well functioning income tax. But if this goal proves elusive, then an alternative tax may offer a second best way of achieving this result.

b) Recognition of situation of firm

Ideally, the taxes should bear some relationship to the firm's ability to pay. While it is only possible to accurately measure this capacity through an income tax, some bases, such as capital, may be related to the profitability of the firm over the medium term, assuming that the firm earns a normal rate of profit. Other taxes, based on more gross measures such as assets or revenues, will impose taxes even when the firm is in a loss making position.

c) Exactly right versus approximately right

Having said this, if the income tax system results in zero tax on a consistent basis, even for profitable firms, then some positive tax may represent a better approximation of reality overall, even if firms are required to pay taxes in years of reduced profits or losses. In order to achieve this result it may be necessary to resort to "rough justice" calculations to avoid the complexity and avoidance possibilities which can make the income tax ineffective.

d) Treatment of transactions

One of the great sources of complexity in taxing financial institutions is the attempt to achieve the "right" result for each transaction. In principle this is a worthy objective given the increasingly precise pricing resulting from the increasingly competitive nature of the financial business. However the result in the income tax is to add complexity, complexity that can often be exploited to reduce tax through tax planning. An alternative tax can avoid this complexity, but ideally it should be designed in a manner which minimises the interference with the efficient pricing of products.

e) Foreign tax credit implications

International tax considerations are increasingly important in the financial sector. Many major capital exporting countries provide relief from double taxation through a system of foreign tax credits, under which taxes to offshore jurisdictions are credited against the tax payable on the underlying income in the home country. This feature can be particularly important for insurance companies, which have traditionally operated through branches, (although there is an increasing tendency to use subsidiaries). Credits are normally restricted to income taxes. A non-income alternative tax will generally not be creditable. The impact of this can be reduced through careful design as discussed below.

f) Conflict with prudential goals

Taxation, by its nature works in the opposite direction to prudential regulation since it reduces the profitability of the industry. Two issues arise in the context of regulation. First, if the tax is not related to income, it may be applied even when the firm is making losses and so will exacerbate any solvency problems being experienced by the company. Second, the taxation of some bases, such as capital, may be viewed as providing a disincentive to the very thing that the regulator is trying to promote.

g) Relationship to VAT

In theory a VAT should apply to the services portion of a financial contract, but not to the savings component. In practice a comprehensive approach to the taxation of financial services has not yet been developed and implemented. Therefore a number of countries have introduced alternative taxes on the financial sector as a replacement of the VAT, rather than as a replacement of the income tax.

Possible Bases

A variety of tax bases have been used to fulfil, at least in part, the objectives of an alternative tax. These possibilities include:

a) Alternative minimum taxes

An alternative minimum tax is based upon a different definition of income that is considered to more closely approximate economic income. Typically a number of provisions, such as accelerated depreciation or a partial exclusion of capital gains from income will be reversed to derive a new, broader tax base. An amount of tax is then computed with respect to this new base. The company then pays the higher of the newly calculated tax and the ordinary income tax.

b) Assets or capital

An industry may be assumed to have a typical return to either assets or capital. A low rate of tax could be applied to this broad base to approximate the tax that would be owing if the firm earned the average rate of return in the industry.

c) Premiums

Many jurisdictions apply taxes on premiums of certain types of insurance products. These are generally considered to be a form of sales tax. In a number of jurisdictions, however the premium tax is treated as a minimum income tax and is payable to the extent that the firm does not pay income tax.

d) Reserves

For insurance companies, reserves are the main constituent of liabilities. A form of tax on the income accruing to these reserves has been implemented in a number of countries to ensure that the funds accumulated to pay future liabilities are subject to tax.

e) Dividend relief systems

Certain dividend relief systems, such as an advanced corporations tax, ensure that tax has been paid at the corporate level when a dividend is paid that will be subject to dividend relief in the hands of the shareholder. Tax is levied on the paying corporation to the extent that it has not been paid under the ordinary income tax. This has some of the effect of a minimum tax triggered by distributions.

f) Transaction taxes

Taxes on transactions, such as stamp duties, are sometimes viewed as a possible supplement to income taxation in situations where this is difficult to levy effectively on the financial sector.

Interaction Between Alternative Tax and Income Tax

In order to act as an alternative tax to the income tax, rather than an additional tax, it is necessary to ensure that no alternative tax is payable when "sufficient" income tax has been paid. This is most easily accomplished by allowing some form of crediting between the two taxes. The goal is to ensure that the taxpayer pays the greater of the regular income tax or the alternative tax. Crediting raises a number of technical issues.

1. Carryovers

In any industry, the level of tax effort can vary from year to year. The property and casualty industry is notoriously cyclical in earnings pattern. It experiences occasional catastrophic claims that can cause substantial losses. In addition, fluctuation of taxes paid can arise from timing differences in methods of accounting, for example between revenue and costs. In this case any tax foregone is simply a deferral and does not represent a permanent reduction in the tax base. In such circumstances, while an alternative tax should be payable at the time the deferral is created, it should be effectively refunded when the deferral is ended. The simplest way of ensuring this result is to allow carry-overs of credits for taxes paid to the extent that they cannot be used in a year.

If an alternative tax is paid in a year then it should be allowed to be carried forward (for some specified length of time) to be offset against any income tax which is paid in the future to the extent that it exceeds the alternative tax payable in that year. In theory, carry-backs could also be allowed, but this is not desirable. It would make the tax system more vulnerable to sudden changes in tax effort by a firm, perhaps in response to a new tax-planning scheme.

2. Credit Trading

Some firms may not be able to use their excess alternative tax credits against income tax payable, if for what ever reason they are not likely to be in an income taxpaying situation for a period of time. In that case there will be an incentive to trade the unused credits to someone who is currently paying income tax, in much the same way that loss companies have found ways to trade unused losses. Rules to stop such trading can be complex.

3. Direction of Crediting

Which tax should be traded against which? In a purely domestic context, it would seem immaterial. When a company is moving in and out of tax-paying status from year to year, this would be the case. On the other hand, when a company moves from a pattern of non-payment to one of payment, or *vice versa*, the order of crediting can impact differently on firms.

Consider a firm with a history of non-payment of income taxes (perhaps due to deficiencies in the income tax law). It will accordingly pay alternative tax in those years. If the alternative tax is to be credited against income tax, then the tax paid in the initial years would be available to be credited against any excess income tax paid when the company starts paying income tax, (subject to the carry forward period). If however, the ordering of crediting is reversed, and the income tax reduces the alternative tax payable, then no relief would be granted with respect to the alternative tax paid in the early years, (unless carry-backs were allowed). One negative result of allowing crediting of the alternative tax against the income tax would be that the revenue benefits of any tightening of a deficient income tax would be delayed since the previous alternative tax paid acts as a form of loss carry forward.

The situation is effectively reversed in a situation where the firm ceases to pay tax. In that case any excess income tax paid eliminates the alternative tax payable. This is good, if the firm is non-taxpaying due to losses, but it reduces the effectiveness of the alternative tax in discouraging new methods of tax avoidance.

The other consideration in determining the order of crediting is the interaction of the alternative tax with the foreign tax mechanisms of the resident countries of non-resident insurers operating in the jurisdiction imposing the alternative tax. As noted above, non-income alternative taxes will generally not generate foreign tax credits. Thus, if taxes in the foreign jurisdiction exceed domestic taxes so that the full amount of domestic income tax is creditable, the total tax will be higher, if the non-income tax is credited against the income tax. In that case, the non-income tax will only generate a deduction against income. This effect is demonstrated in the following table.

Table 21. **Impact of direction of crediting**

	Income tax credited	Non-income tax credited
Source country		
Income	100	100
Non-income tax	30	30
Gross income tax (40%)	40	40
Net income tax	40	10
Total source country tax	40	40
Residence country		
Income	100	70
Gross income tax (40%)	40	28
Foreign tax credit	40	10
Net income tax	0	18
Total tax	40	58

The alternative is to negotiate a tax treaty provision allowing creditability of the non-income tax on the grounds that it is a proxy for an income tax.

Alternative Minimum Taxes

An alternative minimum tax is a parallel calculation to the ordinary income tax that does not contain some of the features that lead to an inappropriate reduction in income tax liability. General alternative minimum taxes such as exists in the United States operate by substituting more stringent provisions for provisions contained in the ordinary income tax which have an element of incentive. The theory being that the incentive is needed to boost the amount of the particular activity, but that overall, everyone should pay at least a minimum amount of tax.

Income-based alternative taxes however are not effective when the underlying reason for the lack of tax is not the provision of identifiable incentives, but rather arises from technical deficiencies in the law. This latter case typifies insurance (non-)taxation. In that case, if a provision could be devised to achieve the desired result, then it would presumably be able to be incorporated into the ordinary income tax. Accordingly, alternative minimum taxes are unlikely to provide an effective response to low taxation effort by insurance companies arising from the inherent complexity of their operations.

Taxes on Assets or Capital

Either assets or capital provide a large stable tax base that is not very prone to tax avoidance activity. Capital in particular is attractive because most insurance companies look to ways to increase their capital to make themselves attractive to prospective policyholders (little chance of non-payment of claims) and to satisfy regulators. The use of assets does give rise to some manipulation at the margin if assets can be held offshore or in non-financial subsidiaries and then leased back. Moreover reinsurance can be used to export either capital or assets out of the taxing jurisdiction.

Another important consideration is the stability of the relationship of the base chosen to the expected income of the firm. If assets are chosen, then it must be assumed that the ratio of income to assets is relatively stable. However for firms which operate in different insurance lines facing different levels of risk, it is likely that the margins earned are related to risk of business. As riskier lines of business should also require higher amounts of capital, capital might provide a better guide to expected income than do assets. Finally, lower levels of capital relative to assets are likely to arise in cases of financial difficulty, and so using capital as the tax base would again be more appropriate. However it is clear that tax would likely still be exigible even when the firm was in a loss making position.

The major criticism of using capital is likely to arise from its conflict with regulatory goal of raising the levels of capital in the companies. The tax is directly on the element of the balance sheet that provides the financial cushion against insolvency.

There are a variety of structural issues that arise when designing such a tax.

The first is which balance sheet items to use, the tax balance sheet or the accounting balance sheet. To the extent that the use of tax preferences giving rise to accelerated deductions is a reason that the ordinary income tax is low, the tax cost of the assets will also be correspondingly low. Therefore using the tax balance sheet might not be effective. There are a number of other advantages in using the regulatory balance sheet of the company. The balance sheet of an insurance company is audited by the regulator and reported to shareholders. It is therefore somewhat less subject to manipulation that would be a special balance sheet that was only used for the purposes of this tax. In addition for both of these uses the company has an incentive to report capital, rather than hide it. Finally, using an existing balance sheet has the advantage of simplicity, for both taxpayers and the tax administration, a useful characteristic when adding an additional tax.

The treatment of investments made in subsidiaries also raises design issues. The problem is to avoid double counting, without giving rise to tax planning activities. If the subsidiary is another company subject to the tax, (*i.e.* a financial institution if the tax applies to other financial institutions or an insurance company if the tax is restricted to that industry), then the capital implicit in the equity held of the subsidiary would be taxed in its hands and so should be deducted from the capital of the parent. On the other hand, equity held in non-financial subsidiaries, should be treated as any other investment as it does not give rise to double counting.

A decision will also need to be made about treatment of foreign assets, if the company operates through offshore branches. In this case, there are two possibilities. Assuming that the goal is to tax domestic income, then the tax could be applied only to domestic assets, or to the share of domestic capital that corresponds to domestic assets. Any alternative tax payable should then only be credited against income tax arising from domestic operations. Alternatively, the tax could be applied on the whole of the assets or capital, in which case it would, in theory, be appropriate to allow credits for foreign income taxes to be offset against the alternative tax. Such crediting would expose the alternative tax to some of the manipulations of foreign tax credits that are one of the reasons that domestic income tax may be inappropriately sheltered.

In some cases the tax is only applied to amounts of capital above a threshold. In such cases, the threshold should be shared among companies in a group. An interesting question would be whether a life and a P&C company that were joined in a group should each be given an individual threshold. [By giving a threshold to each company we would penalise amalgamation if it were allowed. But only allowing one threshold would penalise diversified groups of financial companies.]

A number of OECD countries currently levy such taxes as minimum taxes. Canada applies a minimum tax based upon the capital of a life insurance company, (the tax does not apply to P&C companies although a similar tax does apply to banks). Mexico applies a general assets tax that is creditable against income tax.

Premium Taxes

Most countries apply premium taxes on general insurance. Tax revenues are large and easy to collect. The tax is imposed on the insurer. Brokers (or agents) may have to pay the tax where the policy is underwritten by an insurer that sells insurance through a broker or agent. Rates vary from 2% to 30% of premiums. Premium taxes are low in North America due to retaliatory provisions.[1] Premium taxes are sometimes used to replace sales taxes or VAT. In some cases premium taxes are ear-marked, (premiums on fire insurance may be used as a fire brigade revenue source).

Most EU countries do not levy sales taxes or premium taxes on life insurance policies. This is because life insurance policies are often pension or savings type products with very little or no life insurance. Life insurance policies (particularly deferred annuities and investment bonds) compete with similar products offered by banks, which are not subject to premium taxes. These products are also part of the pension system in many cases and so benefit from a preferential tax treatment. Where there is a tax, the rate is usually low and applies to non-life policies and ordinary life policies (not annuities).

Reinsurance is usually excluded from premium taxes on the basis that tax has already been paid on directly written premiums. As a consequence, inward reinsurance (reinsurance of foreign risks) is exempt from premium taxes.

Premium taxes also represent a potential tax base for an alternative tax, (as has been implemented in Estonia). They are simple to levy as they apply to premiums on all domestic policies written by an insurer. In looking at the P&C industry the main problem with using premiums as a alternative tax base is that the profits of P&C companies is highly cyclical, and so the tax will often be applied in circumstances where the company has low or no profits. In addition, it should be recognised that the tax rules which apply to P&C companies are relatively simple, the major problem being the use of reinsurance, and so an alternative tax directed solely at P&C companies may not be appropriate.

---

1. Most states in America levy penalty taxes on out of state insurers whose home jurisdictions impose premium taxes on their insurers at a rate higher than some threshold (often 2 per cent) even when the tax is imposed uniformly on local and non-resident insurers.

Premium taxes are more problematic when applied to life policies. Life insurance contracts are generally of long duration and can often be considered to be saving vehicles, either implicitly or explicitly. Accordingly, the premiums paid may incorporate significant amounts of what is essentially a payment of principal. Taxation of the principal portion of a life policy would put insurance products at a severe disadvantage relative to competing financial products such as bank deposits. Moreover when viewed as a alternative tax to an income tax, the company profit inherent in a policy relative to the premiums paid with respect to it would vary widely as the amount of savings versus pure insurance varies widely across different insurance policies. Yearly renewable term insurance incorporates almost no savings element, longer term insurance can have a reasonably significant implicit saving component and whole life insurance incorporates a significant explicit savings function.

Taxes Based on Reserves

Reserves represent the major liability of life insurance companies. They also represent a significant source of tax sheltering for insurance companies. As such they could represent a potential target for an alternative tax to reduce the impact of excessive reserve deductions. However, the problems of a high variance of the size of reserves for different policies, (due to the need to reserve for the return of the effective principal component of the premiums that have been received) are the same as for taxes based on premiums.

As noted above, a simple tax on reserves, which taxes a portion of the implicit interest return to the reserve to fund future liabilities can act as an alternative tax to the taxation of the inside build up in the policy at the policyholder level.

Dividend Relief Systems

Many countries operate dividend relief systems, which are intended to relieve the double taxation that would otherwise occur when taxes are paid on income earned at the corporate level and then a second layer of tax is imposed when dividends are paid out to individual shareholders. In some cases, relief from double taxation is given only if corporate level tax is paid or a special tax is imposed on the distribution in lieu of the corporate income tax. In that case, a dividend relief system acts as type of minimum tax on distributions.

Clearly a dividend relief system is an integral structural part of a tax system which would apply to companies in all industries. However, a dividend relief system has some attractive features when considered as a minimum tax as it applies only to firms which have made financial profits, (at least at some point), as they are able to make distributions. At the same time it allows firms to continue to benefit from any tax incentives which they may have earned as long as they keep the funds in the company.

On the other hand, it can be said to allow a firm to delay any tax consequences simply by forgoing dividend payments. Moreover from the point of view of a tax on insurance companies it suffers from a serious structural problem, as many insurance companies are mutual companies which do not have shareholders and so do not pay ordinary dividends. Thus stock insurance companies would be placed under a competitive disadvantage under such a system.

Transaction Taxes

Transaction taxes include many different types of taxes, such as taxes on the value of a transaction, *i.e.* sale of securities or stamp duties, which are set fees for the registration of legal documents. Some jurisdictions impose such taxes as an indirect means of taxing the profits arising in the transaction. In this case, the tax is similar to a sales tax and so could be seen to be a proxy for the taxation of gains arising on behalf of the individual investor. However, such taxes applied to transactions involving financial institutions could be seen as an indirect way of taxing the activity of these companies.

Transaction taxes have a number of serious deficiencies. They are effectively a tax on intermediation that raises its cost. Given the role of intermediation as a basic input in the allocation of capital with an economy, this form of taxation penalises the establishment of an efficient market by increasing the cost of its administration. Moreover, the taxes generally bear no relationship to the profitability of the companies as they may suffer an overall loss from their insurance business even if they are able to make income on the transactions in the security market. Finally, the site of transactions is highly mobile and so transaction taxes can often be avoided, especially by sophisticated financial institutions.

Accordingly, transaction taxes are generally not a large revenue source in OECD countries and the trend has been toward their elimination.

Chapter 14

COMPARISONS OF SELECTED OECD COUNTRIES: PREMIUM TAXES ON INSURANCE COMPANIES[1]

	Premium taxes on general insurance	Premium taxes on life insurance
Australia	0%-21% state fire levies	5% of first year premium (term insurance) 0.05 – 0.1% of sum assured on other life policies
Austria	1%-10%	Health 1% Life and casualty: pension contributions and special life insurance (annuities beginning with retirement): 2.5% short terms life insurance with single premium and benefits paid at once: 11% all other life insurance: 4%
Belgium	1.4%-9.25% (compensatory funds: 0.35%-10%)	4.4% plus 8.86% on employers' contributions of group insurance/pension funds
Canada	1%-4% (5%-15% sales taxes)	Provincial taxes 2% to 4% except annuities and reinsurance – Sales tax in Ontario (8%), Quebec (9%) on group life
Finland	22%	exempt
Germany	2%-15%	Exempt
Ireland	2%	2% plus 0.1% of sum insured
Italy	2.5%-21.25% (comp. funds: 4%-10.5%)	2.5%
Luxembourg	4%-6%	exempt
Mexico	10%	exempt
Netherlands	7%	Exempt
New Zealand	3.8%	Exempt
Portugal	0-13%	Premiums and pension fund contributions (0.08%)
Spain	6%	Exempt
Sweden	None	Group pension 24.26%, Group life (45% of 95% of premiums), No tax on premiums paid to foreign insurer
Switzerland	2.5%-5%	2.5% on redeemable capital life insurance and pension life insurance policies financed by single premiums
United Kingdom	5%	Exempt
United States	3%-4%	State taxes 2% to 3%, except annuities and reinsurance

1. Data in tables updated to October 1999.

GLOSSARY OF TERMS

24th basis (or method)

Is a method for computing an unearned premium reserve. It is computed by combining premiums having the same term (*e.g.* 12, 6 or 3 months, 1 month or any other term), each group being divided by the month in which premiums were written and each premium deemed to have been written in the middle of the month. Accordingly, any 12-month premium written in January will be considered to have been written on January 15 and will therefore provide coverage for 15 days beyond the closing date, *i.e.*, 1/24th of the premium in question. A premium written in December of the same year will be deemed to take effect as of 15 December and provide coverage beyond the closing date of 23/24th of the said premium.

Accident and sickness insurance

Various kinds of health insurance offering benefits for loss of income or expenses resulting from accidental injury, sickness, or from accidental death.

Accidental death benefit

A payment of a specified sum, in addition to the regular death benefit, in the event of the death of the insured by accident or by accidental means.

Acquisition costs

Costs incurred in acquiring insurance business such as agents' and brokers' commissions, medical and selection expenses, issue expenses, premium taxes, etc.

Actuarial assumptions

1) The mortality, morbidity, interest, expenses, and other forecasts used to calculate premium rates and reserves.
2) In pension planning, the assumptions that actuaries make in the areas of investment earnings, mortality, plan expenses, salary levels, and employee turnover. These assumptions affect the amount of the annual contribution that is necessary to adequately fund a defined benefit pension plan.

Actuary

An expert who applies assumptions about the probability of future events, *i.e.* mortality, morbidity, interest rates, expenses, lapse rates and other forecasts to calculate the premiums which are required to fund a given type of insurance policy and to compute reserves to be set aside by insurance companies to cover future liabilities. A person in this job applies the theory of probability to calculate mortality rates, morbidity rates, lapse rates, premium rates, policy reserves, and other values

Annuitant

The person in receipt of annuity payments.

Annuity, certain

An annuity that provides benefits payable for a specified period of time regardless of the lifespan of the annuitant.

Annuity

A contract under which an annuitant pays a principal amount in exchange for a series of payments to be received at regular intervals. Annuities may be for fixed periods or for the life of the annuitant and/or dependants and may be immediate or deferred.

Beneficiary

The person to whom the proceeds of a life insurance policy are assigned.

Benefits

The indemnities or payments specified in the insurance contracts. These include, for life insurance, policy benefits, waiver of premiums in event of disability, payments of income because of permanent disability, and double indemnity.

Broker

A salesperson who sells insurance products for more than one insurance company.

Capital redemption

Business whereby in return for one or more premiums, a sum or series of sums is to become payable to the insured in the future, without reference to the death or survival of any life insured.

Captive insurance company

An insurance subsidiary formed to provide insurance to a controlling company. All types of companies can form captive insurers. Captives are often formed in jurisdictions outside of the jurisdiction of the controlling company for both regulatory and tax reasons.

Cash (surrender) value

In a life insurance policy, the amount of money that the policyholder will receive if they allow the policy to lapse or if they cancel the coverage and surrender the policy to the insurance company. Generally it is some percentage of the total premiums paid on the policy minus the expenses and the costs of pure insurance associated with the policy. Cash surrender values are often offered for whole life, endowment and universal life policies.

Catastrophe

A single event which gives rise to a very large claim or series of claims. Examples include earthquake, hurricanes, oil spills and other similar events. Catastrophe policies are usually reinsured and may give rise to special contingency reserves.

Ceding company (cedant)

In a reinsurance transaction, the insurer that purchases reinsurance to cover all or part of those risks that it does not wish to retain in full.

Cession

The act of ceding; or a parcel or unit of insurance that a company cedes to a reinsurer.

Claim (or loss)

The amount payable under an insurance policy following an occurrence covered by the policy.

Coinsurance

A reinsurance contract under which the ceding company remits a portion of the premium received from the insured, minus a proportionate share of the commission and other expenses. In return, the reinsurer agrees to pay the ceding company a proportionate part of any claims or other benefits arising from the policy.

Commission

The remuneration paid to an agent or broker for the introduction of business, usually in the form of a percentage of the premium. An allowance made by the reinsurer for part or all of a ceding company's acquisition and other costs. It may also include a profit factor.

Contingency reserve

A voluntary reserve established by an insurance company to help pay any unusual and unexpectedly large claim amounts.

Convertible term insurance

A form of term life insurance that allows the policyholder to convert the term insurance policy to a whole life policy without providing further evidence of insurability.

Decreasing term insurance

A form of term life insurance where the amount of coverage decreases over the term of the policy.

Deferred annuity

An annuity contract under which premiums are contributed immediately, but the annuity payments are postponed (deferred) into the future. Often a form of pension.

Direct writer

An insurer that sells insurance directly to the public and to non-insurance commercial and industrial enterprises.

Disability insurance

A type of health insurance which provides periodic income replacement payments to a person who is unable to work due to some form of disability.

Dividend

(1) A payment of excess accumulation of value in a policy to the owner of an individual participating life insurance policy. Such a dividend is paid out of an insurer's surplus and could be considered to be a return of premium or a distribution of accumulated income. Also called a policy dividend or a policyholder dividend.

(2) A residual amount in excess of payments made for claims that is returned to a group policyholder whose claims experience is better than had been expected when the premium was calculated. Also called experience rating refund.

Endowment insurance

Endowment insurance is similar to whole life insurance in that it builds up capital that is returned to the policyholder and provides life insurance cover over its term. It differs, however, in that it provides for a payment to be made to the policyholder without the surrender of the policy at a fixed date in the future. Therefore it contains an explicit savings function for the policyholder. The fixed payment will often be converted into an annuity at time of maturity.

Equalisation reserve

This valuation adjustment smoothes out non-life profits for certain seasonal or cyclical risks, such as hail, natural disasters, space or nuclear risks, pollution liability or credit insurance; or for an insurer entire portfolio.

Face amount (sum insured)

The amount stated on the face of the policy that will be paid on the death of the life insured or at the maturity of the policy. It does not include additional amounts payable under accidental death or other special provisions, or acquired through the application of policy dividends.

Facultative reinsurance

These contracts are used for very large risks which treaties cannot absorb, and unique risks for which it is difficult to establish a reinsurance treaty. Under this type of contract, a risk is individually offered by the cedant and accepted by reinsurers only when it meets their underwriting criteria.

Group life insurance

Life insurance issued, usually without medical examination, on a group of people under a master contract. It is usually issued to an employer for the benefit of employees. The individual members of the group hold certificates as evidence of their insurance.

Immediate annuity

An annuity contract under which payments begin immediately after the annuity is purchased.

Increasing term insurance

A type of term insurance in which the death benefit of the policy increases over the term of policy, at a fixed rate or linked to some index.

Incurred but not reported (IBNR)

IBNR is estimated on the basis of prior loss experience and, in particular, the claims patterns over several years. Recoveries and subrogation, as well as any salvage, are taken into account in the estimation. IBNR will include claims not yet received and claims which take substantial time to be manifested.

Inside build-up (or roll up)

The amount of interest after the deduction of administration expenses which is credited to a life insurance policy through the calculation of the policy reserve.

Insurance

An risk management arrangement against individual loss in which policyholders pay premiums to create a fund from which the individuals can be compensated for losses caused by events such as fire, accident, illness, or death. Risks are pooled among the policyholders and a portion may be shifted to an insurance company.

Investment valuation reserve

Broadly represents the value of a company's assets over and above its recognised liabilities to policyholders, shareholders and others. It may appear explicitly in the office's accounts as an appropriation of surplus, or implicitly where assets are given a book value below market value.

Investment risk

Investment risk stem from the large size of the assets managed by the insurer on behalf of policyholders or beneficiaries, which are subject to requirements as to profitability, safety, availability and matching and must be equivalent to the insurer's technical commitments.

Key-person insurance

Life insurance purchased by a business on an important employee, partner or shareholder whose death or disability would cause financial loss to the company.

Lapse

The termination of an insurance policy because premiums were not paid when due.

Law of large numbers

A theory of probability that states that the mean of a series of observed results will approximate mathematically expected population mean as the number of observations increases.

Life annuity with period certain

A life annuity under which, if the annuitant dies within a fixed time period, payments will be continued to a designated payee until the end of the period.

Life annuity

Annuity payments that continue for the life of the annuitant.

Life Insurance in Force

The sum of the face amounts, plus dividend additions, of life insurance policies outstanding at a given time. Additional amounts payable under accidental death or other special provisions are not included.

Life insurance

Insurance that provides protection against the economic loss caused by the death of the person insured.

Margin for adverse deviations

An additional (prudent) amount added to (or subtracted from) assumptions which increase the valuation of a reserve.

Mark to market

The valuation of assets and liabilities to their market value.

Mathematical reserves

The actuarially calculated assessment of a company's obligations to policyholders, consisting essentially of the difference between the present value of anticipated benefits to policyholders and the present value of future premiums.

Moral hazard

The problem that the purchase of insurance coverage might cause the insured to forego risk reducing actions that they would otherwise undertake, thus increasing the probability of an insurable event.

Morbidity

The rate of death, disease or other loss of health in a population.

Mortality cost

The assumed cost of insurance for any year is the contribution necessary from each policy to meet the net death benefits anticipated during that year. It may be calculated by multiplying the net amount at risk at the beginning of the policy year by the death rate (as shown by the mortality table) at the age attained by the insured at the beginning of the policy year.

Mutual insurance company

An insurance company without stockholders, whose surplus is held by the insurance company on behalf of its policyholders.

Net amount at risk

The death benefit of a life insurance policy minus the policy's reserve at the end of the policy year.

Net level premium reserve

A form of life insurance reserve under which the reserve is calculated under the assumption that premiums are received in equal amounts to cover future benefit payments.

Non-proportional reinsurance treaty

A treaty whereby the reinsurer agrees to pay some or all of the excess over an agreed amount in respect of a loss incurred by the cedant. Premiums are calculated independently.

Participating (par) policy

A form of life insurance policy under which the excess accumulation of funds over a pre-determined return may be paid to the policyholder in the form of policy dividends.

Policy loan

A loan that is made to a life insurance policyholder by an insurer. A policy loan is secured by a policy's cash value and cannot exceed the cash value. When the policy benefits are paid, the amount of any outstanding policy loan made against the policy is deducted from the benefits.

Non-participating (non-par) policy

A form of life insurance policy in which the policyholder's benefits are fixed in advance and not adjustable under the experience of the policy category.

Policyholder

The person or party who owns an insurance policy. The policyholder is not necessarily the person whose life is insured. In some cases a distinction is made between a policyholder and a policyowner with the policyholder being a company or organisation that owns a group insurance contract and a policyowner being the holder of an individual contract. The terms policyholder and policyowner are frequently used interchangeably. In this paper, policyholder is used in all cases.

Premium tax

A form of sales tax paid on premiums received on insurance policies. Rates vary widely across jurisdictions and types of risks, being generally low in North America and higher for some types of P&C insurance in Europe.

Premium

The consideration the insurer receives for the accepting the risk of liability under an insurance policy.

Proportional reinsurance treaty

A reinsurance treaty where both parties share the risk proportionally with regard to the premiums and losses.

Stock insurance company

An insurance company in the form of a joint stock company owned by its shareholders.

Quota share

A type of reinsurance plan whereby the insurer cedes a specified percentage of the relevant premium to the reinsurer, who in return accepts the same percentage of the corresponding claims.

Reinsurance treaty

A broadly worded statement of the agreement between a reinsurer and a ceding company. The three common types of reinsurance treaties are automatic, facultative, and facultative-obligatory. Usually just called a treaty.

Reinsurance

A transaction between two insurance companies in which one company purchases insurance from the other to cover part or all of the risks that the first company does not wish to retain in full.

Reinsurer

An insurance company that accepts the risk transferred from another insurance company in a reinsurance transaction. Also called the assuming company.

Renewable term insurance

Term insurance under which the policyholder has the right to renew the insurance coverage at the end of the policy without further evidence of insurability.

Reserve for unexpired risks

In general, the reserve for unexpired risks is an amount of premiums that have to be allocated to following year or subsequent years in order to cover risks to be incurred on contracts in force on the valuation date. In the EEC, it refers to a provision that supplements the unearned premium reserve (provision) if accounting or statistical data suggests the latter may be inadequate to cover risks and risk management expenses after the financial year.

Reserve (or technical provision)

The amount of assets set aside in a special liability account to pay future claims. The yearly change in assets yields a charge against income.

Retention

The net amount of risk retained by a ceding company net of reinsurance.

Retrospective-rating arrangement

An alternative funding method for a group insurance contract whereby the insurer collects only a percentage (often between 90 % and 95 %) of the premium from the policyholder at the beginning of the premium-paying period and collects the rest of the premium at the end of the period, unless the group's claim experience is better than expected and the additional premium therefore is not owed. With this system the policyholder retains control of part of the premium for a longer time than with the traditional system

Salvage value

The value of recoveries from the insured.

Surplus

The actuarial surplus of a life company is that part of the fund over and above the sum of its liabilities. Holders of "with-profits" policies are entitled to a share in the surplus, usually by way of a reversionary bonus added periodically to and payable with the sum assured.

Term insurance

A life insurance policy that provides coverage for a fixed number of years.

Tort

A tort is a civil wrong resulting in injury to a person or property.

Underwriting profit

Money earned by an insurance company in its underwriting operation as distinguished from money earned in the investment of assets.

Unearned premium

That portion of the premium on a policy or group of policies, which applies to the time that the policy still has to run. The company earns its premium as the policy term goes on. The rest is unearned.

Valuation basis

The particular set of assumptions and conventions upon which the actuary bases his valuation of the liability.

Whole life insurance

Provides protection for the lifetime of the person insured. The term is sometimes used to embrace ordinary life, straight life and limited payment life insurance – it can be "with" or "with-out" profits.

Zillmerization

A modification of the net premium reserve method of valuing a long-term policy – it increases the part of future premiums for which credit is taken so as to allow for initial expenses.

BIBLIOGRAPHY

Council Directive of 19 December 1991,
  on the annual accounts and consolidated accounts of insurance undertakings (91/674/EEC), Official Journal of the European Commission, No. L 374/7

Cross-Boarder Reinsurance: Current Issues,
  Karl Walsh, Stephen C. Eldridge, North American Conference on Insurance Taxation (1993), Hartford Institute of Insurance Taxation, Centre for Tax Education and Research.

Financial Reporting for Property and Casualty Insurers,
  A Research Study, The Canadian Institute of Chartered Accountants, 1974.

Fundamentals of Risk and Insurance,
  4th Edition, Emmett J. Vaughan, University of Iowa, 1986.

Glossary of Policy Terms,
  Centre for co-operation with Non-Members, OECD 1999.

Insurance Statistics Yearbook,
  1990-1997, OECD, 1999.

Liberalisation of International Insurance Operations: Cross-Border Trade and Establishment of Foreign Branches,
  OECD 1999.

Reinsurance Tax Consideration, Karl Walsh, Stephen C. Eldridge, International Conference on Insurance Taxation (1990), Hartford Institute of Insurance Taxation, Centre for Tax Education and Research.

Significant Developments in the Taxation of Insurance Companies and their Products, 1993-1994,
  Hartford Institute of Insurance Taxation, Centre for Tax Education and Research.

Reinsurance,
  Revised Edition, Edited and published by Robert W. Strain, CLU, CPCU, Strain Publishing and Seminar Inc.

Taxation of Household Savings,
  OECD, 1994.

The Determination of Underwriting Profits: The New Zealand Approach,
  Keith G. Jones, A.M.P. Society, Asia-Pacific Conference on Insurance Taxation (1990), Hartford Institute of Insurance Taxation, Centre for Tax Education and Research.

OECD TAX POLICY STUDIES

1. Taxing Powers of State and Local Government (November 1999)
2. Tax Burdens: Alternative Measures (December 1999)
3. Taxing Insurance Companies
4. Corporate Tax Incentives for Foreign Direct Investment
5. Tax Ratios: A Critical Study (Forthcoming)
6. Tax Policy in OECD Countries (Forthcoming)

OECD PUBLICATIONS, 2, rue André-Pascal, 75775 PARIS CEDEX 16
PRINTED IN FRANCE
(23 2001 02 1 P) ISBN 92-64-18345-0 – No. 51717 2001